OLD MOORI

Horoscope and Astral Diary

SAGITTARIUS

OLD MOORE'S

HOROSCOPE AND ASTRAL DIARY

SAGITTARIUS

foulsham
LONDON • NEW YORK • TORONTO • SYDNEY

W. Foulsham & Co. Ltd
for Foulsham Publishing Ltd
The Old Barrel Store, Drayman's Lane, Marlow, Bucks SL7 2FF

Foulsham books can be found in all good bookshops and direct from
www.foulsham.com

ISBN: 978-0-572-04688-0

A CIP record for this book is available from the British Library

Printed in Great Britain by Martins The Printers, Berwick-upon-Tweed

CONTENTS

INTRODUCTION

Astrology has been a part of life for centuries now, and no matter how technological our lives become, it seems that it never diminishes in popularity. For thousands of years people have been gazing up at the star-clad heavens and seeing their own activities and proclivities reflected in the movement of those little points of light. Across centuries countless hours have been spent studying the way our natures, activities and decisions seem to be paralleled by their predictable movements. Old Moore, a time-served veteran in astrological research, continues to monitor the zodiac and has produced the Astral Diary for 2018, tailor-made to your own astrological makeup.

Old Moore's Astral Diary is unique in its ability to get the heart of your nature and to offer you the sort of advice that might come from a trusted friend. It enables you to see in a day-by-day sense exactly how the planets are working for you. The diary section advises how you can get the best from upcoming situations and allows you to plan ahead successfully. There's also room on each daily entry to record your own observations or appointments.

While other popular astrology books merely deal with your astrological 'Sun sign', the Astral Diaries go much further. Every person on the planet is unique and Old Moore allows you to access your individuality in a number of ways. The front section gives you the chance to work out the placement of the Moon at the time of your birth and to see how its position has set an important seal on your overall nature. Perhaps most important of all, you can use the Astral Diary to discover your Rising Sign. This is the zodiac sign that was appearing over the Eastern horizon at the time of your birth and is just as important to you as an individual as is your Sun sign.

It is the synthesis of many different astrological possibilities that makes you what you are and with the Astral Diaries you can learn so much. How do you react to love and romance? Through the unique Venus tables and the readings that follow them, you can learn where the planet Venus was at the time of your birth. It is even possible to register when little Mercury is 'retrograde', which means that it appears to be moving backwards in space when viewed from the Earth. Mercury rules communication, so be prepared to deal with a few setbacks in this area when you see the sign ☿. The Astral Diary will be an interest and a support throughout the whole year ahead.

Old Moore extends his customary greeting to all people of the Earth and offers his age-old wishes for a happy and prosperous period ahead.

THE ESSENCE OF SAGITTARIUS

Exploring the Personality of Sagittarius the Archer

(23RD NOVEMBER – 21ST DECEMBER)

What's in a sign?

Sagittarius is ruled by the large, expansive planet Jupiter, which from an astrological perspective makes all the difference to this happy-go-lucky and very enterprising zodiac sign. This is the sign of the Archer and there is a very good reason for our ancient ancestors having chosen the half-man, half-horse figure with its drawn bow. Not only are Sagittarians fleet-footed like a horse, but the remarks they make, like the arrow, go right to the target.

You love contentious situations and rarely shy away from controversy. With tremendous faith in your own abilities you are not easily kept down, and would usually find it relatively simple to persuade others to follow your course. Though you are born of a Fire sign, you are not as bullying as Aries can be, or as proud as a Leo. Despite this you do have a Fire-sign temper and can be a formidable opponent once you have your dander up.

You rarely choose to take the long route to any destination in life, preferring to drive forward as soon as your mind is made up. Communication comes easy to you and you add to your stock of weapons good intuitive insight and a capacity for brinkmanship that appears to know no bounds. At your best you are earnest, aspiring and honourable, though on the other side of the coin Sagittarians can make the best con artists of all!

What you hate most is to be discouraged, or for others to thwart your intentions. There is a slight tendency for you to use others whilst you are engaging in many of the schemes that are an intrinsic part of your life, though you would never deliberately hurt or offend anyone.

Sagittarian people are natural lovers of fun. When what is required is a shot of enthusiasm, or an immediacy that can cut right through the middle of any red tape, it is the Archer who invariably ends up in charge. When others panic, you come into your own, and you have an ability to get things done in a quarter of the expected time. Whether they are completed perfectly, however, is a different matter altogether.

Sagittarius resources

Sagittarians appear to be the natural conjurors of the zodiac. The stage magician seems to draw objects from thin air, and it often appears that the Archer is able to do something similar. This is an intriguing process to observe, but somewhat difficult to explain. Sagittarians seem to be able to get directly to the heart of any matter, and find it easy to circumnavigate potential difficulties. Thus they achieve objectives that look impossible to observers – hence the conjuring analogy.

Just as the biblical David managed to defeat Goliath with nothing more than a humble pebble and a sling, Sagittarius also goes seemingly naked into battle. The Archer relies on his or her natural wit, together with a fairly instinctive intelligence, a good deal of common sense and a silver tongue. The patient observer must inevitably come to the conclusion that what really matters isn't what the Sagittarian can do, but how much they manage to get others to undertake on their behalf. In other words, people follow your lead without question. This quality can be one of your best resources and only fails when you have doubt about yourself, which fortunately is very rarely.

If other signs could sell refrigerators to Eskimos, you could add a deep-freeze complete with ice tray! This is one of the reasons why so many Archers are engaged in both advertising and marketing. Not only do you know what people want, you also have an instinctive ability to make them want whatever it is you have on offer.

It is likely that you would see nothing remotely mysterious about your ability to peer through to the heart of any matter. In the main you would refer to this as 'gut reaction', despite the fact that it looks distinctly magical to those around you. Fortunately this is part of your mystique, and even if you should choose to take someone for a complete ride, it is doubtful that they would end up disliking you as a result. You don't set out to be considered a genius, and you manage to retain the common touch. This is extremely important, for those with whom you have contacts actively want to help you because you are a 'regular guy'.

Beneath the surface

People tend to be very complicated. Untangling their motives in any given situation is rarely easy. Psychologists have many theories regarding the working of the human psyche and philosophers have struggled with such matters for thousands of years. Clearly none of these people were looking at the zodiac sign of Sagittarius. Ask the average Archer why they did this or that thing and the chances are that you will get a reply something very similar to 'Well, it seemed like a good idea at the time'.

While many people might claim to be uncomplicated, at heart you genuinely are. Complications are something you try to avoid, even though some of your deals in life might look like a roll of barbed wire to those around you. In the main you keep your objectives as simple as possible. This is one of the reasons why it isn't particularly difficult for you to circumnavigate some of the potential pitfalls – you simply won't recognise that they exist. Setting your eyes on the horizon you set off with a jaunty step, refusing to acknowledge problems and, when necessary, sorting them out on the way.

Your general intention is to succeed and this fact permeates just about every facet of your life. Satisfaction doesn't necessarily come for you from a job well done, because the word 'well' in this context often isn't especially important. And when you have one task out of the way, you immediately set your sights on something else. Trying to figure out exactly why you live your life in the way you do, your psychological imperatives and ultimate intentions, costs you too much time, so you probably don't indulge in such idle speculation at all.

You have a warm heart and always want the best for everyone. It almost never occurs to you that other people don't think about things in the way you might and you automatically assume that others will be only too pleased to follow your lead. In the main you are uncomplicated, don't indulge in too many frills and fancies and speak your mind. There really isn't much difference between what you do in life, and what you think about your actions. This is not to infer that you are shallow, merely that you don't see much point in complicating the obvious with too much internal musing.

One of the main reasons why people like you so much is because the 'what you see is what you get' adage is more true in your case than in any other.

Making the best of yourself

Always on the go and invariably looking for a new challenge, it isn't hard to see how Sagittarius makes the best of itself. This is a dynamic, thrusting sign, with a thirst for adventure and a great ability to think on its feet. As a child of Sagittarius you need the cut and thrust of an exciting life in order to show your true mettle. It doesn't do for you to sit around inactive for any length of time and any sort of enforced lay-off is likely to drive you to distraction.

In a career situation your natural proclivities show through, so it's best for you to be in some position which necessitates decision making on a moment-by-moment basis. Production-line work or tasks that involve going over the same ground time and again are not really your forte, though you are certainly not afraid of hard work and can labour on regardless towards any objective – just as long as there is a degree of excitement on the way.

Socially speaking you probably have many friends, and that's the way you like things to be. You need to know that people rate you highly, and will usually be on hand to offer the sort of advice that is always interesting, but probably not totally reasoned. It's a fact that you think everyone has the same ability to think on their feet that typifies your nature, and you trust everyone instinctively – at least once.

In love you need the sort of relationship that allows a degree of personal freedom. You can't be fettered and so have to be your own person under all situations. You are kind and attentive, though sometimes get carried away with the next grand scheme and so you need an understanding partner. Archers should not tie themselves down too early in life and are at their best surrounded by those who love the dynamism and difficult-to-predict qualities exemplified by this zodiac sign.

Most important of all you need to be happy with your lot. Living through restricted or miserable times takes its toll. Fortunately these are few in your life, mainly because of the effort you put into life yourself.

The impressions you give

You must be doing something right because it's a fact that Sagittarius represents one of the most instinctively liked zodiac signs. There are many reasons for this state of affairs. For starters you will always do others a good turn if it's possible. It's true that you are a bit of a rogue on occasions, but that only endears you to the sort of individuals with whom you choose to share your life. You are always the first with a joke, even under difficult circumstances, and you face problems with an open mind and a determination to get through them. On the way you acquire many friends, though in your case many 'acquaintances' might be nearer the mark. This is a situation of your own choosing and though you have so much to recommend you to others, it's a fact that you keep really close ties to the absolute minimum.

Some people might think you rather superficial and perhaps an intellectual lightweight. If so, this only comes about because they don't understand the way your mind works. All the same it is your own nature that leads a few individuals to these conclusions. You can skip from one subject to another, are an insatiable flirt in social situations and love to tell funny stories. 'Depth' isn't really your thing and that means that you could appear to lower the tone of conversations that are getting too heavy for your liking. You do need to be the centre of attention most of the time, which won't exactly endear you to others who have a similar disposition.

People know that you have a temper, like all Fire signs. They will also realise that your outbursts are rare, short-lived and of no real note. You don't bear a grudge and quickly learn that friends are more useful than enemies under any circumstance.

You come across as the capricious, bubbly, lively, likeable child of the zodiac and under such circumstances it would be very difficult for anyone to find fault with you for long. Often outrageous, always interesting and seldom down in the dumps – it's hard to see how you could fail to be loved.

The way forward

It might be best to realise, right from the outset, that you are not indestructible. Deep inside you have all the same insecurities, vulnerabilities and paranoia that the rest of humanity possesses. As a Sagittarian it doesn't do to dwell on such matters, but at least the acknowledgement might stop you going over the edge sometimes. You come from a part of the zodiac that has to be active and which must show itself in the best possible light all the time, and that's a process that is very demanding.

In the main, however, you relish the cut and thrust of life and it is quite likely that you already have the necessary recipe for happiness and success. If you don't, then you are involved in a search that is likely to be both interesting and rewarding, because it isn't really the objective that matters to you but rather the fun you can have on the way.

Be as honest as you can with those around you, though without losing that slightly roguish charm that makes you so appealing. At the same time try to ensure that your own objectives bear others in mind. You can sometimes be a little fickle and, in rare circumstances, unscrupulous. At heart though, you have your own moral convictions and would rarely do anyone a bad turn. On the contrary, you do your best to help those around you, and invariably gain in popularity on the way.

Health-wise you are probably fairly robust but you can run your nervous system into the ground on occasions. There are times when a definite routine suits you physically, but this doesn't always agree with your mental make-up, which is essentially driving and demanding. The peaks and troughs of your life are an inevitable part of what makes you tick, and you would be a poorer person without them.

Explaining yourself is not generally difficult, and neither is the search for personal success, even if you keep looking beyond it to even greater achievements further down the road. Being loved is important, despite the fact that you would deny this on occasions. Perhaps you don't always know yourself as well as you might, though since you are not an inveterate deep thinker it is likely that this is not a problem to you.

If you are already an adult, it's likely the path you are presently following is the one for you. That doesn't mean to say that you will keep to it, or find it universally rewarding. You find new promise in each day, and that's the joy of Sagittarius.

SAGITTARIUS ON THE CUSP

Old Moore is often asked how astrological profiles are altered for those people born at either the beginning or the end of a zodiac sign, or, more properly, on the cusps of a sign. In the case of Sagittarius this would be on the 23rd of November and for two or three days after, and similarly at the end of the sign, probably from the 19th to the 21st of December. In this year's Astral Diaries, once again, Old Moore sets out to explain the differences regarding cuspid signs.

The Scorpio Cusp – November 23rd to 25th

You could turn out to be one of the most well-liked people around, especially if you draw heavily from the more positive qualities of the two zodiac signs that have the most profound part to play in your life. Taken alone the Sagittarian is often accused of being rather too flighty. Sagittarians are often guilty of flirting and sometimes fall foul of people who take a more serious view of life in general. The presence in your make-up of the much deeper and more contemplative sign of Scorpio brings a quiet and a sense of reserve that the Sagittarian nature sometimes lacks. Although you like to have a good time and would be more than willing to dance the night away, you are probably also happy enough when the time comes to go home. Family means much to you and you have a great sensitivity to the needs of those around you. What makes all the difference is that you not only understand others, but you have the potential to take practical steps to help them.

You are probably not quite the workaholic that the Archer alone tends to be and can gain rest and relaxation, which has to be good for you in the longer term. You don't lack the ability to be successful but your level of application is considered, less frenetic and altogether more ordered. It's true that some confusion comes into your life from time to time, but you have the resources to deal with such eventualities, and you do so with a smile on your face most of the time. People would warm to you almost instantly and you are likely to do whatever you can to support family members and friends.

Often sinking into a dream world if you feel threatened, some of the achievements that are second nature to the Sagittarian are left on the shelf for a while. There are times when this turns out to be a blessing, if only because your actions are more considered. Personality clashes with others are less likely with this combination and Sagittarius also modifies the slightly moody qualities that come with Scorpio alone. More methodical in every way than the usual Archer, in many situations you are a good combination of optimist and pessimist.

The Capricorn Cusp – December 19th to 21st

The fact that comes across almost immediately with the Capricorn cusp of Sagittarius is how very practical you tend to be. Most of you would be ideal company on a desert island, for a number of reasons. Firstly you are quite self-contained, which Sagittarius taken alone certainly is not. You would soon get your head round the practical difficulties of finding food and shelter, and would be very happy to provide these necessities for your companions too. Unlike the typical Sagittarian you do not boast and probably do not come across as being quite so overbearing as the Archer seems to be. For all this you are friendly, chatty, love to meet many different and interesting types and do whatever you can to be of assistance to a world which is all the better for having you in it.

There is less of a tendency for you to worry at a superficial level than Sagittarius alone is inclined to do, mainly because long periods of practical application bring with them a contemplative tendency that Sagittarius sometimes lacks. In love you tend to be quite sincere, even if the slightly fickle tendencies of the Archer do show through now and again. Any jealousy that is levelled at you by your partner could be as a result of your natural attractiveness, which you probably don't seek. Fairly comfortable in almost any sort of company, you are at your best when faced with individuals who have something intelligent and interesting to say. As a salesperson you would be second to none, but it would be essential for you to believe absolutely in the product or service you were selling.

Almost any sort of work is possible in your case, though you wouldn't take too kindly to being restricted in any way, and need the chance to show what your practical nature is worth, as well as your keen perception and organisational abilities. What matters most for you at work is that you are well liked by others and that you manage to maintain a position of control through inspiring confidence. On a creative level, the combination of Sagittarius and Capricorn would make you a good sculptor, or possibly a natural landscape gardener.

SAGITTARIUS AND ITS ASCENDANTS

The nature of every individual on the planet is composed of the rich variety of zodiac signs and planetary positions that were present at the time of their birth. Your Sun sign, which in your case is Sagittarius, is one of the many factors when it comes to assessing the unique person you are. Probably the most important consideration, other than your Sun sign, is to establish the zodiac sign that was rising over the eastern horizon at the time that you were born. This is your Ascending or Rising sign. Most popular astrology fails to take account of the Ascendant, and yet its importance remains with you from the very moment of your birth, through every day of your life. The Ascendant is evident in the way you approach the world, and so, when meeting a person for the first time, it is this astrological influence that you are most likely to notice first. Our Ascending sign essentially represents what we appear to be, while the Sun sign is what we feel inside ourselves.

The Ascendant also has the potential for modifying our overall nature. For example, if you were born at a time of day when Sagittarius was passing over the eastern horizon (this would be around the time of dawn) then you would be classed as a double Sagittarius. As such, you would typify this zodiac sign, both internally and in your dealings with others. However, if your Ascendant sign turned out to be an Earth sign, such as Taurus, there would be a profound alteration of nature, away from the expected qualities of Sagittarius.

One of the reasons why popular astrology often ignores the Ascendant is that it has always been rather difficult to establish. Old Moore has found a way to make this possible by devising an easy-to-use table, which you will find on page 125 of this book. Using this, you can establish your Ascendant sign at a glance. You will need to know your rough time of birth, then it is simply a case of following the instructions.

For those readers who have no idea of their time of birth it might be worth allowing a good friend, or perhaps your partner, to read through the section that follows this introduction. Someone who deals with you on a regular basis may easily discover your Ascending sign, even though you could have some difficulty establishing it for yourself. A good understanding of this component of your nature is essential if you want to be aware of that 'other person' who is responsible for the way you make contact with the world at large. Your Sun sign, Ascendant sign, and the other pointers in this book will, together, allow you a far better understanding of what makes you tick as an individual. Peeling back the different layers of your astrological make-up can be an enlightening experience, and the Ascendant may represent one of the most important layers of all.

Sagittarius with Sagittarius Ascendant

You are very easy to spot, even in a crowd. There is hardly a more dynamic individual to be found anywhere in the length and breadth of the zodiac. You know what you want from life and have a pretty good idea about how you will get it. The fact that you are always so cocksure is a source of great wonder to those around you, but they can't see deep inside, where you are not half as certain as you appear to be. In the main you show yourself to be kind, attentive, caring and a loyal friend. To balance this, you are determined and won't be thwarted by anything.

You keep up a searing pace through life and sometimes find it difficult to understand those people who have slightly less energy. In your better moments you understand that you are unique and will wait for others to catch up. Quite often you need periods of rest in order to recharge batteries that run down through over-use, but it doesn't take you too long to get yourself back on top form. In matters of the heart you can be slightly capricious, but you are a confident lover who knows the right words and gestures. If you are ever accused of taking others for granted you might need to indulge in some self-analysis.

Sagittarius with Capricorn Ascendant

The typical Sagittarian nature is modified for the better when Capricorn is part of the deal. It's true that you manage to push forward progressively under most circumstances, but you also possess staying power and can work long and hard to achieve your objectives, most of which are carefully planned in advance. Few people have the true measure of your nature, for it runs rather deeper than appears to be the case on the surface. Routines don't bother you as much as would be the case for Sagittarius when taken alone, and you don't care if any objective takes weeks, months or even years to achieve. You are very fond of those you take to, and prove to be a capable friend, even when things get tough.

In love relationships you are steadfast and reliable, and yet you never lose the ability to entertain. Yours is a dry sense of humour which shows itself to a multitude of different people and which doesn't evaporate, even on those occasions when life gets tough. It might take you a long time to find the love of your life, but when you do there is a greater possibility of retaining the relationship for a long period. You don't tend to inherit money, but you can easily make it for yourself, though you don't worry too much about the amount. On the whole you are self-sufficient and sensible.

Sagittarius with Aquarius Ascendant

There is an original streak to your nature which is very attractive to the people with whom you share your life. Always different, ever on the go and anxious to try out the next experiment in life, you are interested in almost everything and yet deeply attached to almost nothing. Everyone you know thinks that you are a little 'odd', but you probably don't mind them believing this because you know it to be true. In fact it is possible that you positively relish your eccentricity, which sets you apart from the common herd and means that you are always going to be noticed.

Although it may seem strange with this combination of Air and Fire, you can be distinctly cool on occasions, have a deep and abiding love of your own company now and again, and won't easily be understood. Love comes fairly easily to you but there are times when you are accused of being self-possessed, self-indulgent and not willing enough to fall in line with the wishes of those around you. Despite this you walk on and on down your own path. At heart you are an extrovert and you love to party, often late into the night. Luxury appeals to you, though it tends to be of the transient sort. Travel could easily play a major and a very important part in your life.

Sagittarius with Pisces Ascendant

A very attractive combination this, because the more dominant qualities of the Archer are somehow mellowed-out by the caring Water-sign qualities of the Fishes. You can be very outgoing, but there is always a deeper side to your nature that allows others to know that you are thinking about them. Few people could fall out with either your basic nature or your attitude to the world at large, even though there are depths to your personality that may not be easily understood. You are capable, have a good executive ability and can work hard to achieve your objectives, even if you get a little disillusioned on the way. Much of your life is given over to helping those around you and there is a great tendency for you to work for and on behalf of humanity as a whole. A sense of community is brought to most of what you do and you enjoy co-operation.

Although you have the natural Sagittarian ability to attract people to you, the Pisces half of your nature makes you just a little more reserved in personal matters than might otherwise be the case. More careful in your choices than either sign taken alone, you still have to make certain that your motivations when commencing a personal relationship are the right ones. You love to be happy, and to offer gifts of happiness to others.

Sagittarius with Aries Ascendant

What a lovely combination this can be, for the devil-may-care aspects of Sagittarius lighten the load of a sometimes too serious Aries interior. Everything that glistens is not gold, though it's hard to convince you of the fact because, to mix metaphors, you can make a silk purse out of a sow's ear. Almost everyone loves you, and in return you offer a friendship that is warm and protective, but not as demanding as sometimes tends to be the case with the Aries type. Relationships may be many and varied and there is often more than one major attachment in the life of those holding this combination. You can bring a breath of spring to any relationship, though you need to ensure that the person concerned is capable of keeping up with the hectic pace of your life.

It may appear from time to time that you are rather too trusting for your own good, though deep inside you are very astute, and it seems that almost everything you undertake works out well in the end. This has nothing to do with native luck and is really down to the fact that you are much more calculating than might appear to be the case at first sight. As a parent you are protective, yet offer sufficient room for self-expression.

Sagittarius with Taurus Ascendant

A dual nature is evident here, and if it doesn't serve to confuse you it will certainly be a cause of concern to many of the people with whom you share your life. You like to have a good time and are a natural party-goer. On such occasions you are accommodating, chatty and good to know. But contrast this with the quieter side of Taurus, which is directly opposed to your Sagittarian qualities. The opposition of forces is easy for you to deal with because you inhabit your own body and mind all the time, but it's far less easy for friends and relatives to understand. As a result, on those occasions when you decide that, socially speaking, enough is enough, you will need to explain the fact to the twelve people who are waiting outside your door with party hats and whoopee cushions.

Confidence to do almost anything is not far from the forefront of your mind and you readily embark on adventures that would have some types flapping about in horror. Here again, it is important to realise that we are not all built the same way and that gentle coaxing is sometimes necessary to bring others round to your point of view. If you really have a fault, it could be that you are so busy being your own, rather less than predictable self, that you fail to take the rest of the world into account.

Sagittarius with Gemini Ascendant

'Tomorrow is another day!' This is your belief and you stick to it. There isn't a brighter and more optimistic soul to be found than you and almost everyone you come into contact with is touched by the fact. Dashing about from one place to another, you manage to get more things done in one day than most other people would achieve in a week. Of course this explains why you are so likely to wear yourself out and it means that frequent periods of absolute rest are necessary if you are to remain truly healthy and happy. Sagittarius makes you brave and sometimes a little headstrong, so you need to curb your natural enthusiasm while you stop to think about the consequences of your actions.

It's not really certain if you do 'think' in the accepted sense of the word, because the lightning qualities of both these signs mean that your reactions are second to none. However, you are not indestructible and you put far more pressure on yourself than would often be sensible. Routines are not your thing at all, and many of you manage to hold down two or more jobs at once. It might be an idea to stop and smell the flowers on the way, and you could certainly do with putting your feet up much more than you do. However, you probably won't still be reading this passage because you will have something far more important to do!

Sagittarius with Cancer Ascendant

You have far more drive, enthusiasm and get-up-and-go than would seem to be the case for Cancer when taken alone, but all of this is tempered with a certain quiet compassion that probably makes you the best sort of Sagittarian too. It's true that you don't like to be on your own or to retire in your shell quite as much as the Crab usually does, though there are, even in your case, occasions when this is going to be necessary. Absolute concentration can sometimes be a problem to you, though this is hardly likely to be the case when you are dealing with matters relating to your home or family, both of which reign supreme in your thinking. Always loving and kind, you are a social animal and enjoy being out there in the real world, expressing the deeper opinions of Cancer much more readily than would often be the case with other combinations relating to the sign of the Crab.

Personality is not lacking and you tend to be very popular, not least because you are the fountain of good and practical advice. You want to get things done and retain a practical approach to most situations which is the envy of many other people. As a parent you are second to none, combining common sense, dignity and a sensible approach. To balance this you stay young enough to understand children.

Sagittarius with Leo Ascendant

Above and beyond anything else you are naturally funny, and this is an aspect of your nature that will bring you intact through a whole series of problems that you manage to create for yourself. Chatty, witty, charming, kind and loving, you personify the best qualities of both these signs, whilst also retaining the Fire-sign ability to keep going, long after the rest of the party has gone home to bed. Being great fun to have around, you attract friends in the way that a magnet attracts iron filings. Many of these will be casual connections but there will always be a nucleus of deep, abiding attachments that may stay around you for most of your life.

You don't often suffer from fatigue, but on those occasions when you do there is ample reason to stay still for a while and to take stock of situations. Routines are not your thing and you like to fill your life with variety. It's important to do certain things right, however, and staying power is something that comes with age, assisted by the Fixed quality of Leo. Few would lock horns with you in an argument, which you always have to win. In a way you are a natural debator but you can sometimes carry things too far if you are up against a worthy opponent. You have the confidence to sail through situations that would defeat others.

Sagittarius with Virgo Ascendant

This is a combination that might look rather odd at first sight because these two signs have so very little in common. However, the saying goes that opposites attract, and in terms of the personality you display to the world this is especially true in your case. Not everyone understands what makes you tick but you try to show the least complicated face to the world that you can manage to display. You can be deep and secretive on occasions, and yet at other times you can start talking as soon as you climb out of bed and never stop until you are back there again. Inspirational and spontaneous, you take the world by storm on those occasions when you are free from worries and firing on all cylinders. It is a fact that you support your friends, though there are rather more of them than would be the case for Virgo taken on its own, and you don't always choose them as wisely as you might.

There are times when you display a temper, and although Sagittarius is incapable of bearing a grudge, the same cannot be said for Virgo, which has a better memory than the elephant. For the best results in life you need to relax as much as possible and avoid overheating that powerful and busy brain. Virgo gives you the ability to concentrate on one thing at once, a skill you should encourage.

Sagittarius with Libra Ascendant

A very happy combination this, with a great desire for life in all its forms and a need to push forward the bounds of the possible in a way that few other zodiac sign connections would do. You don't like the unpleasant or ugly in life and yet you are capable of dealing with both if you have to. Giving so much to humanity, you still manage to retain a degree of individuality that would surprise many, charm others, and please all.

On the reverse side of the same coin you might find that you are sometimes accused of being fickle, but this is only an expression of your need for change and variety, which is intrinsic to both these signs. True, you have more of a temper than would be the case for Libra when taken on its own, but such incidents would see you up and down in a flash and it is almost impossible for you to bear a grudge of any sort. Routines get on your nerves and you are far happier when you can please yourself and get ahead at your own pace, which is quite fast.

As a lover you can make a big impression and most of you will not go short of affection in the early days, before you choose to commit yourself. Once you do, there is always a chance of romantic problems, but these are less likely when you have chosen carefully in the first place.

Sagittarius with Scorpio Ascendant

There are many gains with this combination, and most of you reading this will already be familiar with the majority of them. Sagittarius offers a bright and hopeful approach to life, but may not always have the staying power and the patience to get what it really needs. Scorpio, on the other hand, can be too deep for its own good, is very self-seeking on occasions and extremely giving to others. Both the signs have problems when taken on their own, and, it has to be said, double the difficulties when they come together. But this is not usually the case. Invariably the presence of Scorpio slows down the over-quick responses of the Archer, whilst the inclusion of Sagittarius prevents Scorpio from taking itself too seriously.

Life is so often a game of extremes, when all the great spiritual masters of humanity have indicated that a 'middle way' is the path to choose. You have just the right combination of skills and mental faculties to find that elusive path, and can bring great joy to yourself and others as a result. Most of the time you are happy, optimistic, helpful and a joy to know. You have mental agility, backed up by a stunning intuition, which itself would rarely let you down. Keep a sense of proportion and understand that your depth of intellect is necessary in order to curb the more flighty aspects of Scorpio.

THE MOON AND THE PART IT PLAYS IN YOUR LIFE

In astrology the Moon is probably the single most important heavenly body after the Sun. Its unique position, as partner to the Earth on its journey around the solar system, means that the Moon appears to pass through the signs of the zodiac extremely quickly. The zodiac position of the Moon at the time of your birth plays a great part in personal character and is especially significant in the build-up of your emotional nature.

Sun Moon Cycles

The first lunar cycle deals with the part the position of the Moon plays relative to your Sun sign. I have made the fluctuations of this pattern easy for you to understand by means of a simple cyclic graph. It appears on the first page of each 'Your Month At A Glance', under the title 'Highs and Lows'. The graph displays the lunar cycle and you will soon learn to understand how its movements have a bearing on your level of energy and your abilities.

Your Own Moon Sign

Discovering the position of the Moon at the time of your birth has always been notoriously difficult because tracking the complex zodiac positions of the Moon is not easy. This process has been reduced to three simple stages with Old Moore's unique Lunar Tables. A breakdown of the Moon's zodiac positions can be found from page 28 onwards, so that once you know what your Moon Sign is, you can see what part this plays in the overall build-up of your personal character.

If you follow the instructions on the next page you will soon be able to work out exactly what zodiac sign the Moon occupied on the day that you were born and you can then go on to compare the reading for this position with those of your Sun sign and your Ascendant. It is partly the comparison between these three important positions that goes towards making you the unique individual you are.

HOW TO DISCOVER YOUR MOON SIGN

This is a three-stage process. You may need a pen and a piece of paper but if you follow the instructions below the process should only take a minute or so.

STAGE 1 First of all you need to know the Moon Age at the time of your birth. If you look at Moon Table 1, on page 26, you will find all the years between 1920 and 2018 down the left side. Find the year of your birth and then trace across to the right to the month of your birth. Where the two intersect you will find a number. This is the date of the New Moon in the month that you were born. You now need to count forward the number of days between the New Moon and your own birthday. For example, if the New Moon in the month of your birth was shown as being the 6th and you were born on the 20th, your Moon Age Day would be 14. If the New Moon in the month of your birth came after your birthday, you need to count forward from the New Moon in the previous month. If you were born in a Leap Year, remember to count the 29th February. You can tell if your birth year was a Leap Year if the last two digits can be divided by four. Whatever the result, jot this number down so that you do not forget it.

STAGE 2 Take a look at Moon Table 2 on page 27. Down the left hand column look for the date of your birth. Now trace across to the month of your birth. Where the two meet you will find a letter. Copy this letter down alongside your Moon Age Day.

STAGE 3 Moon Table 3 on page 27 will supply you with the zodiac sign the Moon occupied on the day of your birth. Look for your Moon Age Day down the left hand column and then for the letter you found in Stage 2. Where the two converge you will find a zodiac sign and this is the sign occupied by the Moon on the day that you were born.

Your Zodiac Moon Sign Explained

You will find a profile of all zodiac Moon Signs on pages 28 to 31, showing in yet another way how astrology helps to make you into the individual that you are. In each daily entry of the Astral Diary you can find the zodiac position of the Moon for every day of the year. This also allows you to discover your lunar birthdays. Since the Moon passes through all the signs of the zodiac in about a month, you can expect something like twelve lunar birthdays each year. At these times you are likely to be emotionally steady and able to make the sort of decisions that have real, lasting value.

Moon Table I

YEAR	OCT	NOV	DEC	YEAR	OCT	NOV	DEC	YEAR	OCT	NOV	DEC
1920	12	10	10	1953	8	6	6	1986	3	2	1/30
1921	1/30	29	29	1954	26	25	25	1987	22	21	20
1922	20	19	18	1955	15	14	14	1988	10	9	9
1923	10	8	8	1956	4	2	2	1989	29	28	28
1924	28	26	26	1957	23	21	21	1990	18	17	17
1925	17	16	15	1958	12	11	10	1991	8	6	6
1926	6	5	5	1959	2/31	30	29	1992	25	24	24
1927	25	24	24	1960	20	19	18	1993	15	14	14
1928	14	12	12	1961	9	8	7	1994	5	3	2
1929	2	1	1/30	1962	28	27	26	1995	24	22	22
1930	20	19	19	1963	17	15	15	1996	11	10	10
1931	11	9	9	1964	5	4	4	1997	31	30	29
1932	29	27	27	1965	24	22	22	1998	20	19	18
1933	19	17	17	1966	14	12	12	1999	8	8	7
1934	8	7	6	1967	3	2	1/30	2000	27	26	25
1935	27	26	25	1968	22	21	20	2001	17	16	15
1936	15	14	13	1969	10	9	9	2002	6	4	4
1937	4	3	2	1970	1/30	29	28	2003	25	24	23
1938	23	22	21	1971	19	18	17	2004	12	11	11
1939	12	11	10	1972	8	6	6	2005	2	1	1/31
1940	1/30	29	28	1973	26	25	25	2006	21	20	20
1941	20	19	18	1974	15	14	14	2007	11	9	9
1942	10	8	8	1975	5	3	3	2008	29	28	27
1943	29	27	27	1976	23	21	21	2009	18	17	16
1944	17	15	15	1977	12	11	10	2010	8	8	6
1945	6	4	4	1978	2/31	30	29	2011	27	25	25
1946	24	23	23	1979	20	19	18	2012	15	13	12
1947	14	12	12	1980	9	8	7	2013	4	2	2
1948	2	1	1/30	1981	27	26	26	2014	22	22	1
1949	21	20	19	1982	17	15	15	2015	12	11	20
1950	11	9	9	1983	6	4	4	2016	30	29	29
1951	1/30	29	28	1984	24	22	22	2017	20	18	18
1952	18	17	17	1985	14	12	12	2018	09	07	07

Table 2

DAY	NOV	DEC
1	e	i
2	e	i
3	e	m
4	f	m
5	f	n
6	f	n
7	f	n
8	f	n
9	f	n
10	f	n
11	f	n
12	f	n
13	g	n
14	g	n
15	g	n
16	g	n
17	g	n
18	g	n
19	g	n
20	g	n
21	g	n
22	g	n
23	i	q
24	i	q
25	i	q
26	i	q
27	i	q
28	i	q
29	i	q
30	i	q
31	–	q

Table 3

M/D	e	f	g	i	m	n	q
0	SC	SC	SC	SA	SA	SA	CP
1	SC	SC	SA	SA	SA	CP	CP
2	SC	SA	SA	CP	CP	CP	AQ
3	SA	SA	CP	CP	CP	AQ	AQ
4	SA	CP	CP	CP	AQ	AQ	PI
5	CP	CP	AQ	AQ	AQ	PI	PI
6	CP	AQ	AQ	AQ	AQ	PI	AR
7	AQ	AQ	PI	PI	PI	AR	AR
8	AQ	PI	PI	PI	PI	AR	AR
9	AQ	PI	PI	AR	AR	TA	TA
10	PI	AR	AR	AR	AR	TA	TA
11	PI	AR	AR	TA	TA	TA	GE
12	AR	TA	TA	TA	TA	GE	GE
13	AR	TA	TA	GE	GE	GE	GE
14	TA	GE	GE	GE	GE	CA	CA
15	TA	TA	TA	GE	GE	GE	CA
16	TA	GE	GE	GE	CA	CA	CA
17	GE	GE	GE	CA	CA	CA	LE
18	GE	GE	CA	CA	CA	LE	LE
19	GE	CA	CA	CA	LE	LE	LE
20	CA	CA	CA	LE	LE	LE	VI
21	CA	CA	LE	LE	LE	VI	VI
22	CA	LE	LE	VI	VI	VI	LI
23	LE	LE	LE	VI	VI	VI	LI
24	LE	LE	VI	VI	VI	LI	LI
25	LE	VI	VI	LI	LI	LI	SC
26	VI	VI	LI	LI	LI	SC	SC
27	VI	LI	LI	SC	SC	SC	SA
28	LI	LI	LI	SC	SC	SC	SA
29	LI	LI	SC	SC	SA	SA	SA

AR = Aries, TA = Taurus, GE = Gemini, CA = Cancer, LE = Leo, VI = Virgo, LI = Libra, SC = Scorpio, SA = Sagittarius, CP = Capricorn, AQ = Aquarius, PI = Pisces

MOON SIGNS

Moon in Aries

You have a strong imagination, courage, determination and a desire to do things in your own way and forge your own path through life.

Originality is a key attribute; you are seldom stuck for ideas although your mind is changeable and you could take the time to focus on individual tasks. Often quick-tempered, you take orders from few people and live life at a fast pace. Avoid health problems by taking regular time out for rest and relaxation.

Emotionally, it is important that you talk to those you are closest to and work out your true feelings. Once you discover that people are there to help, there is less necessity for you to do everything yourself.

Moon in Taurus

The Moon in Taurus gives you a courteous and friendly manner, which means you are likely to have many friends.

The good things in life mean a lot to you, as Taurus is an Earth sign that delights in experiences which please the senses. Hence you are probably a lover of good food and drink, which may in turn mean you need to keep an eye on the bathroom scales, especially as looking good is also important to you.

Emotionally you are fairly stable and you stick by your own standards. Taureans do not respond well to change. Intuition also plays an important part in your life.

Moon in Gemini

You have a warm-hearted character, sympathetic and eager to help others. At times reserved, you can also be articulate and chatty: this is part of the paradox of Gemini, which always brings duplicity to the nature. You are interested in current affairs, have a good intellect, and are good company and likely to have many friends. Most of your friends have a high opinion of you and would be ready to defend you should the need arise. However, this is usually unnecessary, as you are quite capable of defending yourself in any verbal confrontation.

Travel is important to your inquisitive mind and you find intellectual stimulus in mixing with people from different cultures. You also gain much from reading, writing and the arts but you do need plenty of rest and relaxation in order to avoid fatigue.

Moon in Cancer

The Moon in Cancer at the time of birth is a fortunate position as Cancer is the Moon's natural home. This means that the qualities of compassion and understanding given by the Moon are especially enhanced in your nature, and you are friendly and sociable and cope well with emotional pressures. You cherish home and family life, and happily do the domestic tasks. Your surroundings are important to you and you hate squalor and filth. You are likely to have a love of music and poetry.

Your basic character, although at times changeable like the Moon itself, depends on symmetry. You aim to make your surroundings comfortable and harmonious, for yourself and those close to you.

Moon in Leo

The best qualities of the Moon and Leo come together to make you warmhearted, fair, ambitious and self-confident. With good organisational abilities, you invariably rise to a position of responsibility in your chosen career. This is fortunate as you don't enjoy being an 'also-ran' and would rather be an important part of a small organisation than a menial in a large one.

You should be lucky in love, and happy, provided you put in the effort to make a comfortable home for yourself and those close to you. It is likely that you will have a love of pleasure, sport, music and literature. Life brings you many rewards, most of them as a direct result of your own efforts, although you may be luckier than average and ready to make the best of any situation.

Moon in Virgo

You are endowed with good mental abilities and a keen receptive memory, but you are never ostentatious or pretentious. Naturally quite reserved, you still have many friends, especially of the opposite sex. Marital relationships must be discussed carefully and worked at so that they remain harmonious, as personal attachments can be a problem if you do not give them your full attention.

Talented and persevering, you possess artistic qualities and are a good homemaker. Earning your honours through genuine merit, you work long and hard towards your objectives but show little pride in your achievements. Many short journeys will be undertaken in your life.

Moon in Libra

With the Moon in Libra you are naturally popular and make friends easily. People like you, probably more than you realise, you bring fun to a party and are a natural diplomat. For all its good points, Libra is not the most stable of astrological signs and, as a result, your emotions can be a little unstable too. Therefore, although the Moon in Libra is said to be good for love and marriage, your Sun sign and Rising sign will have an important effect on your emotional and loving qualities.

You must remember to relate to others in your decision-making. Co-operation is crucial because Libra represents the 'balance' of life that can only be achieved through harmonious relationships. Conformity is not easy for you because Libra, an Air sign, likes its independence.

Moon in Scorpio

Some people might call you pushy. In fact, all you really want to do is to live life to the full and protect yourself and your family from the pressures of life. Take care to avoid giving the impression of being sarcastic or impulsive and use your energies wisely and constructively.

You have great courage and you invariably achieve your goals by force of personality and sheer effort. You are fond of mystery and are good at predicting the outcome of situations and events. Travel experiences can be beneficial to you.

You may experience problems if you do not take time to examine your motives in a relationship, and also if you allow jealousy, always a feature of Scorpio, to cloud your judgement.

Moon in Sagittarius

The Moon in Sagittarius helps to make you a generous individual with humanitarian qualities and a kind heart. Restlessness may be intrinsic as your mind is seldom still. Perhaps because of this, you have a need for change that could lead you to several major moves during your adult life. You are not afraid to stand your ground when you know your judgement is right, you speak directly and have good intuition.

At work you are quick, efficient and versatile and so you make an ideal employee. You need work to be intellectually demanding and do not enjoy tedious routines.

In relationships, you anger quickly if faced with stupidity or deception, though you are just as quick to forgive and forget. Emotionally, there are times when your heart rules your head.

Moon in Capricorn

The Moon in Capricorn makes you popular and likely to come into the public eye in some way. The watery Moon is not entirely comfortable in the Earth sign of Capricorn and this may lead to some difficulties in the early years of life. An initial lack of creative ability and indecision must be overcome before the true qualities of patience and perseverance inherent in Capricorn can show through.

You have good administrative ability and are a capable worker, and if you are careful you can accumulate wealth. But you must be cautious and take professional advice in partnerships, as you are open to deception. You may be interested in social or welfare work, which suit your organisational skills and sympathy for others.

Moon in Aquarius

The Moon in Aquarius makes you an active and agreeable person with a friendly, easy-going nature. Sympathetic to the needs of others, you flourish in a laid-back atmosphere. You are broad-minded, fair and open to suggestion, although sometimes you have an unconventional quality which others can find hard to understand.

You are interested in the strange and curious, and in old articles and places. You enjoy trips to these places and gain much from them. Political, scientific and educational work interests you and you might choose a career in science or technology.

Money-wise, you make gains through innovation and concentration and Lunar Aquarians often tackle more than one job at a time. In love you are kind and honest.

Moon in Pisces

You have a kind, sympathetic nature, somewhat retiring at times, but you always take account of others' feelings and help when you can.

Personal relationships may be problematic, but as life goes on you can learn from your experiences and develop a better understanding of yourself and the world around you.

You have a fondness for travel, appreciate beauty and harmony and hate disorder and strife. You may be fond of literature and would make a good writer or speaker yourself. You have a creative imagination and may come across as an incurable romantic. You have strong intuition, maybe bordering on a mediumistic quality, which sets you apart from the mass. You may not be rich in cash terms, but your personal gifts are worth more than gold.

SAGITTARIUS IN LOVE

Discover how compatible in love you are with people from the same and other signs of the zodiac. Five stars equals a match made in heaven!

Sagittarius meets Sagittarius

Although perhaps not the very best partnership for Sagittarius, this must rank as one of the most eventful, electrifying and interesting of the bunch. They will think alike, which is often the key to any relationship but, unfortunately, they may be so busy leading their own lives that they don't spend much time together. Their social life should be something special, and there could be lots of travel. However, domestic responsibilities need to be carefully shared and the family might benefit from a helping hand in this area. Star rating: ****

Sagittarius meets Capricorn

Any real problem here will stem from a lack of understanding. Capricorn is very practical and needs to be constantly on the go, though in a fairly low-key sort of way. Sagittarius is busy too, though always in a panic and invariably behind its deadlines, which will annoy organised Capricorn. Sagittarius doesn't really have the depth of nature that best suits an Earth sign like Capricorn and its flirty nature could upset the sensitive Goat, though its lighter attitude could be cheering, too. Star rating: ***

Sagittarius meets Aquarius

Both Sagittarius and Aquarius are into mind games, which may lead to something of an intellectual competition. If one side is happy to be bamboozled it won't be a problem, but it is more likely that the relationship will turn into a competition which won't auger well for its long-term future. However, on the plus side, both signs are adventurous and sociable, so as long as there is always something new and interesting to do, the match could end up turning out very well. Star rating: **

Sagittarius meets Pisces

Probably the least likely success story for either sign, which is why it scores so low on the star rating. The basic problem is an almost total lack of understanding. A successful relationship needs empathy and progress towards a shared goal but, although both are eager to please, Pisces is too deep and Sagittarius too flighty – they just don't belong on the same planet! As pals, they have more in common and so a friendship is the best hope of success and happiness. Star rating: *

Sagittarius meets Aries

This can be one of the most favourable matches of them all. Both Aries and Sagittarius are Fire signs, which often leads to clashes of will, but this pair find a mutual understanding. Sagittarius helps Aries to develop a better sense of humour, while Aries teaches the Archer about consistency on the road to success. Some patience is called for on both sides, but these people have a natural liking for each other. Add this to growing love and you have a long-lasting combination that is hard to beat. Star rating: *****

Sagittarius meets Taurus

On first impression, Taurus may not like Sagittarius, which may seem brash, and even common, when viewed through the Bull's refined eyes. But, there is hope of success because the two signs have so much to offer each other. The Archer is enthralled by the Taurean's natural poise and beauty, while Taurus always needs more basic confidence, which is no problem to Sagittarius who has plenty to spare. Both signs love to travel. There are certain to be ups and downs, but that doesn't prevent an interesting, inspiring and even exciting combination. Star rating: ***

Sagittarius meets Gemini

A paradoxical relationship this. On paper, the two signs have much in common, but unfortunately, they are often so alike that life turns into a fiercely fought competition. Both signs love change and diversity and both want to be the life and soul of the party. But in life there must always be a leader and a follower, and neither of this pair wants to be second. Both also share a tendency towards infidelity, which may develop into a problem as time passes. This could be an interesting match, but not necessarily successful. Star rating: **

Sagittarius meets Cancer

Although probably not an immediate success, there is hope for this couple. It's hard to see how this pair could get together, because they have few mutual interests. Sagittarius is always on the go, loves a hectic social life and dances the night away. Cancer prefers the cinema or a concert. But, having met, Cancer will appreciate the Archer's happy and cheerful nature, while Sagittarius finds Cancer alluring and intriguing and, as the saying goes, opposites attract. A long-term relationship would focus on commitment to family, with Cancer leading this area. Star rating: ***

Sagittarius meets Leo

An excellent match as Leo and Sagittarius have so much in common. Their general approach to life is very similar, although as they are both Fire signs they can clash impressively! Sagittarius is shallower and more flippant than Leo likes to think of itself, and the Archer will be the one taking emotional chances. Sagittarius has met its match in the Lion's den, as brave Leo won't be outdone by anyone. Financially, they will either be very wealthy or struggling, and family life may be chaotic. Problems, like joys, are handled jointly – and that leads to happiness. Star rating: *****

Sagittarius meets Virgo

There can be some quite strange happenings inside this relationship. Sagittarius and Virgo view life so differently there are always new discoveries. Virgo is much more of a home-bird than Sagittarius, but that won't matter if the Archer introduces its hectic social life gradually. More importantly, Sagittarius understands that it takes Virgo a long time to free its hidden 'inner sprite', but once free it will be fun all the way – until Virgo's thrifty nature takes over. There are great possibilities, but effort is required. Star rating: ***

Sagittarius meets Libra

Libra and Sagittarius are both adaptable signs who get on well with most people, but this promising outlook often does not follow through because each brings out the 'flighty' side of the other. This combination is great for a fling, but when the romance is over someone needs to see to the practical side of life. Both signs are well meaning, pleasant and kind, but are either of them constant enough to build a life together? In at least some cases, the answer would be no. Star rating: ***

Sagittarius meets Scorpio

Sagittarius needs constant stimulation and loves to be busy from dawn till dusk which may mean that it feels rather frustrated by Scorpio. Scorpions are hard workers, too, but they are also contemplative and need periods of quiet which may mean that they appear dull to Sagittarius. This could lead to a gulf between the two which must be overcome. With time and patience on both sides, this can be a lucrative encounter and good in terms of home and family. A variable alliance. Star rating: ***

VENUS: THE PLANET OF LOVE

If you look up at the sky around sunset or sunrise you will often see Venus in close attendance to the Sun. It is arguably one of the most beautiful sights of all and there is little wonder that historically it became associated with the goddess of love. But although Venus does play an important part in the way you view love and in the way others see you romantically, this is only one of the spheres of influence that it enjoys in your overall character.

Venus has a part to play in the more cultured side of your life and has much to do with your appreciation of art, literature, music and general creativity. Even the way you look is responsive to the part of the zodiac that Venus occupied at the start of your life, though this fact is also down to your Sun sign and Ascending sign. If, at the time you were born, Venus occupied one of the more gregarious zodiac signs, you will be more likely to wear your heart on your sleeve, as well as to be more attracted to entertainment, social gatherings and good company. If on the other hand Venus occupied a quiet zodiac sign at the time of your birth, you would tend to be more retiring and less willing to shine in public situations.

It's good to know what part the planet Venus plays in your life, for it can have a great bearing on the way you appear to the rest of the world and since we all have to mix with others, you can learn to make the very best of what Venus has to offer you.

One of the great complications in the past has always been trying to establish exactly what zodiac position Venus enjoyed when you were born, because the planet is notoriously difficult to track. However, I have solved that problem by creating a table that is exclusive to your Sun sign, which you will find on the following page.

Establishing your Venus sign could not be easier. Just look up the year of your birth on the page opposite and you will see a sign of the zodiac. This was the sign that Venus occupied in the period covered by your sign in that year. If Venus occupied more than one sign during the period, this is indicated by the date on which the sign changed, and the name of the new sign. For instance, if you were born in 1950, Venus was in Sagittarius until the 16th December, after which time it was in Capricorn. If you were born before 16th December your Venus sign is Sagittarius, if you were born on or after 16th December, your Venus sign is Capricorn. Once you have established the position of Venus at the time of your birth, you can then look in the pages which follow to see how this has a bearing on your life as a whole.

1920 CAPRICORN / 13.12 AQUARIUS
1921 SCORPIO / 7.12 SAGITTARIUS
1922 SAGITTARIUS / 29.11 SCORPIO
1923 SAGITTARIUS / 2.12 CAPRICORN
1924 LIBRA / 27.11 SCORPIO
1925 CAPRICORN / 6.12 AQUARIUS
1926 SAGITTARIUS / 17.12 CAPRICORN
1927 LIBRA / 9.12 SCORPIO
1928 CAPRICORN / 13.12 AQUARIUS
1929 SCORPIO / 7.12 SAGITTARIUS
1930 SCORPIO
1931 SAGITTARIUS / 2.12 CAPRICORN
1932 LIBRA / 26.11 SCORPIO
1933 CAPRICORN / 6.12 AQUARIUS
1934 SAGITTARIUS / 17.12 CAPRICORN
1935 LIBRA / 10.12 SCORPIO
1936 CAPRICORN / 12.12 AQUARIUS
1937 SCORPIO / 6.12 SAGITTARIUS
1938 SCORPIO
1939 SAGITTARIUS / 1.12 CAPRICORN
1940 LIBRA / 26.11 SCORPIO
1941 CAPRICORN / 6.12 AQUARIUS
1942 SAGITTARIUS / 16.12 CAPRICORN
1943 LIBRA / 10.12 SCORPIO
1944 CAPRICORN / 12.12 AQUARIUS
1945 SCORPIO / 6.12 SAGITTARIUS
1946 SCORPIO
1947 SAGITTARIUS / 1.12 CAPRICORN
1948 LIBRA / 25.11 SCORPIO / 20.12 SAGITTARIUS
1949 CAPRICORN / 7.12 AQUARIUS
1950 SAGITTARIUS / 16.12 CAPRICORN
1951 LIBRA / 10.12 SCORPIO
1952 CAPRICORN / 11.12 AQUARIUS
1953 SCORPIO / 5.12 SAGITTARIUS
1954 SCORPIO
1955 SAGITTARIUS / 30.11 CAPRICORN
1956 LIBRA / 25.11 SCORPIO / 20.12 SAGITTARIUS
1957 CAPRICORN / 8.12 AQUARIUS
1958 SAGITTARIUS / 15.12 CAPRICORN
1959 LIBRA / 10.12 SCORPIO
1960 CAPRICORN / 11.12 AQUARIUS
1961 SCORPIO / 5.12 SAGITTARIUS
1962 SCORPIO
1963 SAGITTARIUS / 30.11 CAPRICORN
1964 LIBRA / 24.11 SCORPIO / 19.12 SAGITTARIUS
1965 CAPRICORN / 8.12 AQUARIUS
1966 SAGITTARIUS / 15.12 CAPRICORN
1967 LIBRA / 10.12 SCORPIO
1968 CAPRICORN / 10.12 AQUARIUS
1969 SCORPIO / 4.12 SAGITTARIUS
1970 SCORPIO
1971 SAGITTARIUS / 29.11 CAPRICORN
1972 LIBRA / 24.11 SCORPIO / 19.12 SAGITTARIUS
1973 CAPRICORN / 9.12 AQUARIUS
1974 SAGITTARIUS / 14.12 CAPRICORN
1975 LIBRA / 9.12 SCORPIO
1976 CAPRICORN / 9.12 AQUARIUS
1977 SCORPIO / 4.12 SAGITTARIUS
1978 SCORPIO
1979 SAGITTARIUS / 28.11 CAPRICORN
1980 SCORPIO / 18.12 SAGITTARIUS
1981 CAPRICORN / 10.12 AQUARIUS
1982 SAGITTARIUS / 14.12 CAPRICORN
1983 LIBRA / 9.12 SCORPIO
1984 CAPRICORN / 9.12 AQUARIUS
1985 SCORPIO / 3.12 SAGITTARIUS
1986 SCORPIO
1987 SAGITTARIUS / 28.11 CAPRICORN
1988 SCORPIO / 18.12 SAGITTARIUS
1989 CAPRICORN / 11.12 AQUARIUS
1990 SAGITTARIUS / 13.12 CAPRICORN
1991 LIBRA / 9.12 SCORPIO
1992 CAPRICORN / 9.12 AQUARIUS
1993 SCORPIO / 3.12 SAGITTARIUS
1994 SCORPIO
1995 SAGITTARIUS / 28.11 CAPRICORN
1996 SCORPIO / 17.12 SAGITTARIUS
1997 CAPRICORN / 12.12 AQUARIUS
1998 SAGITTARIUS / 13.12 CAPRICORN
1999 LIBRA / 9.12 SCORPIO
2000 CAPRICORN / 8.12 AQUARIUS
2001 SCORPIO / 3.12 SAGITTARIUS
2002 SCORPIO
2003 SAGITTARIUS / 28.11 CAPRICORN
2004 SCORPIO / 17.12 SAGITTARIUS
2005 CAPRICORN / 12.12 AQUARIUS
2006 SAGITTARIUS / 13.12 CAPRICORN
2007 LIBRA / 9.12 SCORPIO
2008 CAPRICORN / 8.12 AQUARIUS
2009 SCORPIO / 3.12 AQUARIUS
2010 SCORPIO
2011 SAGITTARIUS / 28.11 CAPRICORN
2012 SCORPIO / 17.12 SAGITTARIUS
2013 SAGITTARIUS / 13.12 CAPRICORN
2014 SAGITTARIUS / 13.12 CAPRICORN
2015 LIBRA / 9.12 SCORPIO
2016 CAPRICORN / 8.12 AQUARIUS
2017 SCORPIO / 3.12 AQUARIUS
2018 SCORPIO

VENUS THROUGH THE ZODIAC SIGNS

Venus in Aries

Amongst other things, the position of Venus in Aries indicates a fondness for travel, music and all creative pursuits. Your nature tends to be affectionate and you would try not to create confusion or difficulty for others if it could be avoided. Many people with this planetary position have a great love of the theatre, and mental stimulation is of the greatest importance. Early romantic attachments are common with Venus in Aries, so it is very important to establish a genuine sense of romantic continuity. Early marriage is not recommended, especially if it is based on sympathy. You may give your heart a little too readily on occasions.

Venus in Taurus

You are capable of very deep feelings and your emotions tend to last for a very long time. This makes you a trusting partner and lover, whose constancy is second to none. In life you are precise and careful and always try to do things the right way. Although this means an ordered life, which you are comfortable with, it can also lead you to be rather too fussy for your own good. Despite your pleasant nature, you are very fixed in your opinions and quite able to speak your mind. Others are attracted to you and historical astrologers always quoted this position of Venus as being very fortunate in terms of marriage. However, if you find yourself involved in a failed relationship, it could take you a long time to trust again.

Venus in Gemini

As with all associations related to Gemini, you tend to be quite versatile, anxious for change and intelligent in your dealings with the world at large. You may gain money from more than one source but you are equally good at spending it. There is an inference here that you are a good communicator, via either the written or the spoken word, and you love to be in the company of interesting people. Always on the look-out for culture, you may also be very fond of music, and love to indulge the curious and cultured side of your nature. In romance you tend to have more than one relationship and could find yourself associated with someone who has previously been a friend or even a distant relative.

Venus in Cancer

You often stay close to home because you are very fond of family and enjoy many of your most treasured moments when you are with those you love. Being naturally sympathetic, you will always do anything you can to support those around you, even people you hardly know at all. This charitable side of your nature is your most noticeable trait and is one of the reasons why others are naturally so fond of you. Being receptive and in some cases even psychic, you can see through to the soul of most of those with whom you come into contact. You may not commence too many romantic attachments but when you do give your heart, it tends to be unconditionally.

Venus in Leo

It must become quickly obvious to almost anyone you meet that you are kind, sympathetic and yet determined enough to stand up for anyone or anything that is truly important to you. Bright and sunny, you warm the world with your natural enthusiasm and would rarely do anything to hurt those around you, or at least not intentionally. In romance you are ardent and sincere, though some may find your style just a little overpowering. Gains come through your contacts with other people and this could be especially true with regard to romance, for love and money often come hand in hand for those who were born with Venus in Leo. People claim to understand you, though you are more complex than you seem.

Venus in Virgo

Your nature could well be fairly quiet no matter what your Sun sign might be, though this fact often manifests itself as an inner peace and would not prevent you from being basically sociable. Some delays and even the odd disappointment in love cannot be ruled out with this planetary position, though it's a fact that you will usually find the happiness you look for in the end. Catapulting yourself into romantic entanglements that you know to be rather ill-advised is not sensible, and it would be better to wait before you committed yourself exclusively to any one person. It is the essence of your nature to serve the world at large and through doing so it is possible that you will attract money at some stage in your life.

Venus in Libra

Venus is very comfortable in Libra and bestows upon those people who have this planetary position a particular sort of kindness that is easy to recognise. This is a very good position for all sorts of friendships and also for romantic attachments that usually bring much joy into your life. Few individuals with Venus in Libra would avoid marriage and since you are capable of great depths of love, it is likely that you will find a contented personal life. You like to mix with people of integrity and intelligence but don't take kindly to scruffy surroundings or work that means getting your hands too dirty. Careful speculation, good business dealings and money through marriage all seem fairly likely.

Venus in Scorpio

You are quite open and tend to spend money quite freely, even on those occasions when you don't have very much. Although your intentions are always good, there are times when you get yourself in to the odd scrape and this can be particularly true when it comes to romance, which you may come to late or from a rather unexpected direction. Certainly you have the power to be happy and to make others contented on the way, but you find the odd stumbling block on your journey through life and it could seem that you have to work harder than those around you. As a result of this, you gain a much deeper understanding of the true value of personal happiness than many people ever do, and are likely to achieve true contentment in the end.

Venus in Sagittarius

You are lighthearted, cheerful and always able to see the funny side of any situation. These facts enhance your popularity, which is especially high with members of the opposite sex. You should never have to look too far to find romantic interest in your life, though it is just possible that you might be too willing to commit yourself before you are certain that the person in question is right for you. Part of the problem here extends to other areas of life too. The fact is that you like variety in everything and so can tire of situations that fail to offer it. All the same, if you choose wisely and learn to understand your restless side, then great happiness can be yours.

Venus in Capricorn

The most notable trait that comes from Venus in this position is that it makes you trustworthy and able to take on all sorts of responsibilities in life. People are instinctively fond of you and love you all the more because you are always ready to help those who are in any form of need. Social and business popularity can be yours and there is a magnetic quality to your nature that is particularly attractive in a romantic sense. Anyone who wants a partner for a lover, a spouse and a good friend too would almost certainly look in your direction. Constancy is the hallmark of your nature and unfaithfulness would go right against the grain. You might sometimes be a little too trusting.

Venus in Aquarius

This location of Venus offers a fondness for travel and a desire to try out something new at every possible opportunity. You are extremely easy to get along with and tend to have many friends from varied backgrounds, classes and inclinations. You like to live a distinct sort of life and gain a great deal from moving about, both in a career sense and with regard to your home. It is not out of the question that you could form a romantic attachment to someone who comes from far away or be attracted to a person of a distinctly artistic and original nature. What you cannot stand is jealousy, for you have friends of both sexes and would want to keep things that way.

Venus in Pisces

The first thing people tend to notice about you is your wonderful, warm smile. Being very charitable by nature you will do anything to help others, even if you don't know them well. Much of your life may be spent sorting out situations for other people, but it is very important to feel that you are living for yourself too. In the main, you remain cheerful, and tend to be quite attractive to members of the opposite sex. Where romantic attachments are concerned, you could be drawn to people who are significantly older or younger than yourself or to someone with a unique career or point of view. It might be best for you to avoid marrying whilst you are still very young.

HOW THE DIAGRAMS WORK

Through the picture diagrams in the Astral Diary I want to help you to plot your year. With them you can see where the positive and negative aspects will be found in each month. To make the most of them, all you have to do is remember where and when!

Let me show you how they work ...

THE MONTH AT A GLANCE

Just as there are twelve separate zodiac signs, so astrologers believe that each sign has twelve separate aspects to life. Each of the twelve segments relates to a different personal aspect. I list them all every month so that their meanings are always clear.

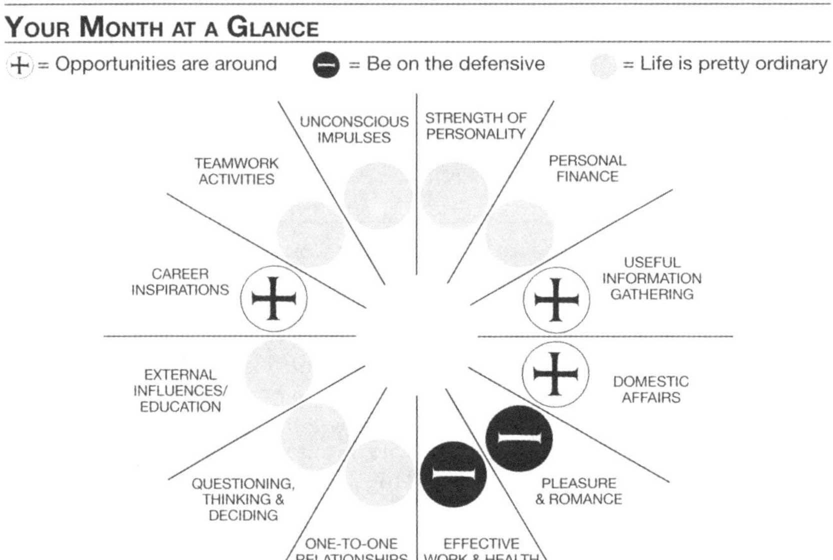

I have designed this chart to show you how and when these twelve different aspects are being influenced throughout the year. When there is a shaded circle, nothing out of the ordinary is to be expected. However, when a circle turns white with a plus sign, the influence is positive. Where the circle is black with a minus sign, it is a negative.

YOUR ENERGY RHYTHM CHART

Below is a picture diagram in which I link your zodiac group to the rhythm of the Moon. In doing this I have calculated when you will be gaining strength from its influence and equally when you may be weakened by it.

If you think of yourself as being like the tides of the ocean then you may understand how your own energies must also rise and fall. And if you understand how it works and when it is working, then you can better organise your activities to achieve more and get things done more easily.

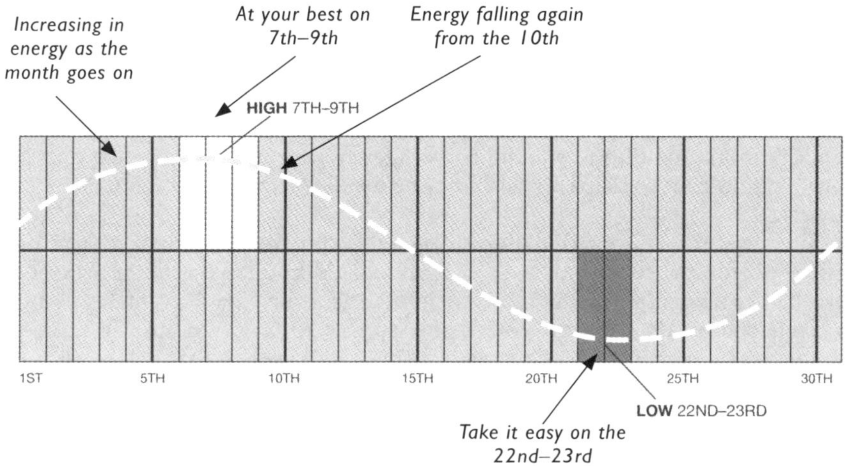

THE KEY DAYS

Some of the entries are in **bold**, which indicates the working of astrological cycles in your life. Look out for them each week as they are the best days to take action or make decisions. The daily text tells you which area of your life to focus on.

MERCURY RETROGRADE

The Mercury symbol (☿) indicates that Mercury is retrograde on that day. Since Mercury governs communication, the fact that it appears to be moving backwards when viewed from the Earth at this time should warn you that your communication skills are not likely to be at their best and you could expect some setbacks.

SAGITTARIUS: YOUR YEAR IN BRIEF

The stars predict that this will be an excellent year for the Archer. Of course, you can't expect everything to go your way but generally, with a little organization and lots of enthusiasm, you get the year started in a sparkling manner. January and February offer good opportunities at work and also bring you closer to achieving a personal objective than you may have been for a year or two. Keep on side with friends who have interesting plans.

March and April may not be the warmest months of the year in terms of weather but that does not really bother you too much. At this time you know exactly what you want and have plenty of Sagittarian confidence to get it. Ask the right questions and don't be afraid to ask again if you don't get the answers you want. You do a lot to help others so may be justified in feeling you are due some payback.

In early summer your thinking is original and focused on change. You may have opportunities for travel, both near and far. Although you might previously have had a tendency to stay close to home, all your Fire-sign vitality is now channelled towards adventure. This also applies to work because it seems as though you are keen to make career changes and also probably take on new responsibilities before May and June are out.

July and August should see you moving about freely, anxious to make a good impression and get on in life. Your powers of communication are especially good and there may be gains to be made when it comes to money. Good luck follows you around so do what you can to make the best of it. Travel is certainly on the agenda throughout this two-month period.

The Sun moves on and the year grows older. September and October should see things slowing down a little. This may be no bad thing because you burn the candle at both ends for most of the time. The autumn gives you the chance to take stock and plan what you want to do next. You may receive some very positive attention and sound advice. Working out who you can trust might be difficult, though.

The last two months of the year, November and December might as well be high summer for all you are concerned because you will be just as lively as if this was the case. On top form in just about every way, you can certainly make the most out of an eventful and quite magical Christmas period. Keep up your efforts right at the end of the year because to do so will lay important groundwork for early next year.

January

2018

Your Month at a Glance

+ = Opportunities are around — = Be on the defensive = Life is pretty ordinary

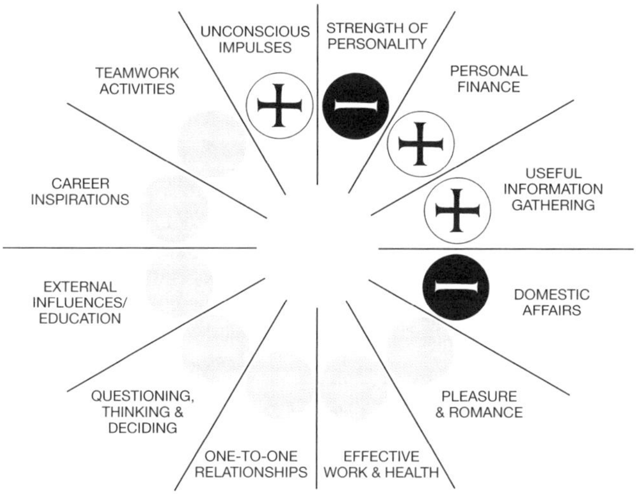

January Highs and Lows

Here I show you how the rhythms of the Moon will affect you this month. Like the tide, your energies and abilities will rise and fall with its pattern. When it is above the centre line, go for it, when it is below, you should be resting.

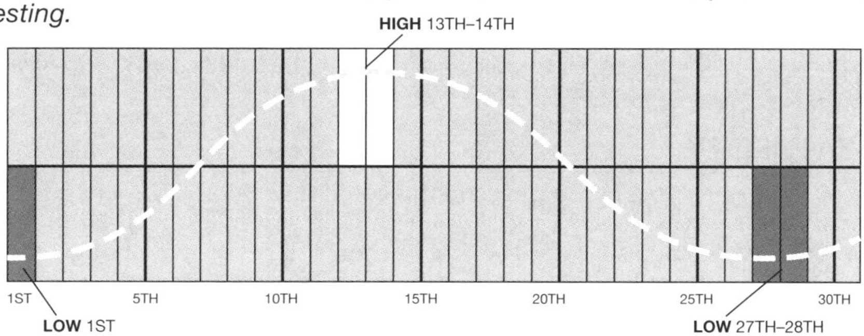

1 MONDAY *Moon Age Day 14 Moon Sign Gemini*

The Moon begins the year in your opposite zodiac sign, bringing the time of the month known as the lunar low. This means you may be a little out of sorts and less inclined to push yourself forward than would usually be the case. Opt for a quiet New Year's Day if you can, but if you have jobs to do ask for some help.

2 TUESDAY *Moon Age Day 15 Moon Sign Cancer*

The way you live, and perhaps also your professional situation, looks likely to change quite significantly during the month of January. The Archer is evolving again, though there is nothing too unusual about this. Friends will prove themselves to be very supportive but relatives might need a little more persuasion.

3 WEDNESDAY *Moon Age Day 16 Moon Sign Cancer*

From an ego point of view you now have the upper hand and your personal charisma has to be experienced to be fully appreciated. Much of what you want can be achieved today but there could be some delays when it comes to monetary payments. Be circumspect for the moment about spending large amounts.

4 THURSDAY *Moon Age Day 17 Moon Sign Leo*

New situations and opportunities of various sorts are likely to take centre-stage in your mind. There are occasions during which it may be necessary to make decisions at lightning speed – though fortunately this is not a problem for Sagittarius. Not everyone relishes your attitude today, but the important people will.

5 FRIDAY *Moon Age Day 18 Moon Sign Leo*

You seem ready for a change of scene and may want to seek out some variety in a general sense. You should be particularly good today at articulating your own ideas, and those of others. All of this adds to your popularity and increases your confidence. You may feel the whole world is ready to give you a hug.

6 SATURDAY *Moon Age Day 19 Moon Sign Virgo*

If you happen to work at the weekend this could turn out to be a very positive sort of day for you. From a social point of view you might feel slightly less inspired than would usually be the case but you will get by well enough when necessary. Root out a family problem and deal with it before the weekend finishes. Friends are supportive.

7 SUNDAY *Moon Age Day 20 Moon Sign Virgo*

It is possible you will have to compensate for your restless frame of mind today. You won't be particularly happy when people or circumstances hold you back and there are times when you will have to bite your tongue instead of getting angry. Progress is still possible but can be complicated.

8 MONDAY *Moon Age Day 21 Moon Sign Libra*

Knowledge and understanding are always important, motivating factors in your life – never more so than right now. Be careful that you don't make your opinions known in a dominating or off-hand manner today because you are so busy dreaming things up you might forget to be as diplomatic as usual.

9 TUESDAY *Moon Age Day 22 Moon Sign Libra*

Gradually the Archer is beginning to achieve a more optimistic frame of mind, which is the way you generally tend to be. Your view of the future is probably clearer now and you can expand your understanding into areas that have been a mystery to you in the past. You remain, as always, ingenious and filled to the brim with good ideas.

10 WEDNESDAY *Moon Age Day 23 Moon Sign Scorpio*

The time is right to sharpen your mind in discussion with the world at large. There are many people around today who seem to have the answers you require and getting them on board is your most important quest. You might have to be charming, humble and very attentive but none of this will cause you the slightest problem.

11 THURSDAY *Moon Age Day 24 Moon Sign Scorpio*

You adapt easily to change and have the ability to switch your viewpoint when necessary. This chameleon-like ability is one of the Archer's most useful weapons and is what sets you apart from the world around you. Conforming to the expectations of others won't always be easy but even if it isn't you can be the consummate actor.

12 FRIDAY *Moon Age Day 25 Moon Sign Scorpio*

You may now experience some changes in existing relationships and you won't want to hang back when it comes to taking centre stage in social gatherings. All things considered this should be a fairly easy-going and happy day, even if nothing extraordinary seems to be happening around you right now.

13 SATURDAY *Moon Age Day 26 Moon Sign Sagittarius*

This is a time for getting ahead and for really putting in all the effort you can. The Moon has returned to your zodiac sign of Sagittarius, bringing that part of the month known as the lunar high. You are filled with enterprise and ambition, and what's more it looks as though everyone is lining up to offer you their help.

14 SUNDAY *Moon Age Day 27 Moon Sign Sagittarius*

Your luck is likely to be in today but you can help yourself no end by capturing the moment when it comes and by using every opportunity to your best advantage. Don't take on everything possible today because it would be far better to achieve a stunning success in one or two specific directions. Avoid unnecessary complications.

15 MONDAY *Moon Age Day 28 Moon Sign Capricorn*

You appear to have a considerable ability to direct your life more constructively now than would sometimes be the case. When something needs to be changed you won't be afraid to take the necessary action and you will be quite happy to bring others on board. Sagittarius is always at its very best when there is an opportunity to share.

16 TUESDAY *Moon Age Day 0 Moon Sign Capricorn*

You may not feel exactly secure with regard to everyday matters, especially if you are at work today. It is vitally important that you avoid rushing your fences. There should be time later in the day to enjoy yourself and it is very important at all stages to safeguard your rather nervy nature.

17 WEDNESDAY *Moon Age Day 1 Moon Sign Capricorn*

The right sort of assistance is inclined to come along when you need it the most today and there are very few people about who would appear to be throwing a spanner in the works. Although you might not really get started on the day until later than you had hoped, the progress you make is swift.

18 THURSDAY *Moon Age Day 2 Moon Sign Aquarius*

Look towards options for growth, which should make themselves very clear around now. This stage of the new working week is likely to be busy but you undertake most jobs with a smile. Don't rush into anything as that will get you into a terrible muddle.

19 FRIDAY *Moon Age Day 3 Moon Sign Aquarius*

Mental strengths are apparent now and many Sagittarians will think themselves unbeatable, especially at work. Avoid pride because, as we know, it often comes before a fall. Be modest and humble enough to admit to yourself and to the world that there are others around who know better than you do.

20 SATURDAY *Moon Age Day 4 Moon Sign Pisces*

You could be in a better position than usual to influence the throw of the dice as far as general good luck is concerned. Meanwhile, others, some of whom have great influence, are noticing your sunny disposition. It has to be said in a professional sense that it's not what you know but who you know that counts today.

21 SUNDAY *Moon Age Day 5 Moon Sign Pisces*

Ingenuity comes to your rescue when it is most important. It is vital that you look at life as thoroughly as you can at the moment and don't dismiss any possibility until you have studied it carefully. Anything that others find difficult to do is grist to the mill for the Archer on this Sunday.

22 MONDAY *Moon Age Day 6 Moon Sign Pisces*

There is little to stand in your way now, on a day that is certainly going to work out well for you. There is a strong possibility that you will be called upon to do things that are not natural to you but such are your capabilities at present that you should be able to deal with such matters without any trouble.

23 TUESDAY *Moon Age Day 7 Moon Sign Aries*

Close and intimate partnerships can make life richer and more interesting at this time. Although you might be feeling somewhat nervy about something, a warm cuddle can set you back on track. This could be a really interesting day, and the more so if you do things that stimulate your intellect.

24 WEDNESDAY *Moon Age Day 8 Moon Sign Aries*

Your influence is very important right now, if only because people generally are taking so much notice of your opinions. That's why it is vitally important to think things through rationally and not to shoot from the hip. If people in the family are arguing, you can pour oil on troubled water.

25 THURSDAY *Moon Age Day 9 Moon Sign Taurus*

You will probably prefer to be on the move whenever possible today. Staying in one place too long is going to be boring and might make it difficult for you to concentrate. This is a frame of mind that Sagittarius adopts now and again and the clear secret is to keep active and interested.

26 FRIDAY *Moon Age Day 10 Moon Sign Taurus*

Don't fall foul of others in arguments right now because to do so will only complicate your life in ways that are not necessary. Keep it light and simple and walk away from disputes of almost any sort. Although you might be seething inside, in a few hours you will be glad of your adult attitude.

27 SATURDAY *Moon Age Day 11 Moon Sign Gemini*

You may feel stifled and forced to compromise more than you would wish and if this is the case you can thank the Moon's present position. Despite the fact that you are unlikely to be on top form there is still margin for success. This is because you know there is more than way to skin a cat and you are the master of alternatives.

28 SUNDAY *Moon Age Day 12 Moon Sign Gemini*

For the second day in a row you may feel as though there are obstacles being placed in the path to success. Fortunately it won't be that far into today before the whole picture begins to change. By the middle of the afternoon you will probably be wondering why you ever allowed yourself to feel pessimistic.

29 MONDAY *Moon Age Day 13 Moon Sign Cancer*

There is a strong emphasis on broadening your horizons now. Not a bad thing at the beginning of a new working week, particularly since there are people around who are only too willing to lend a hand. Stay away from unnecessary complications and always look to the easiest way of solving a problem.

30 TUESDAY *Moon Age Day 14 Moon Sign Cancer*

Though work and practical affairs should provide a very smooth ride today, the same cannot be said regarding personal attachments and family matters. The closer you are to someone, the less likely you are today to understand what makes them tick. Some concentration is called for.

31 WEDNESDAY *Moon Age Day 15 Moon Sign Leo*

Your most rewarding area today is personal attachments. It is true that you are more practical now and less inclined to look on the darker side of life but you still won't be in the mood for pushing forward too hard. The bosom of your family seems to be a good place to be at any time during today.

February

2018

Your Month at a Glance

(+) = Opportunities are around (−) = Be on the defensive ( ) = Life is pretty ordinary

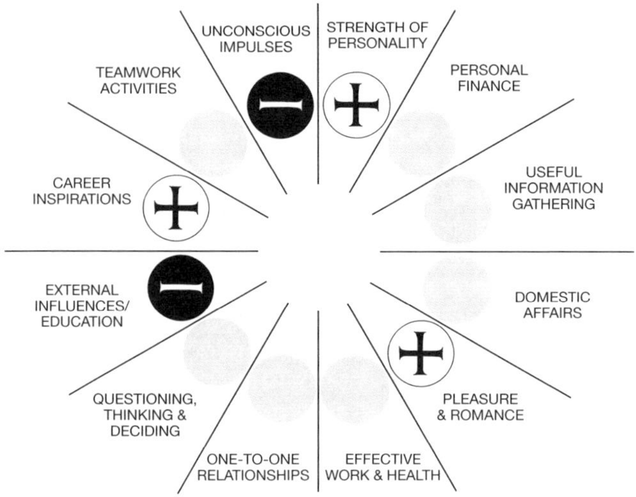

February Highs and Lows

Here I show you how the rhythms of the Moon will affect you this month. Like the tide, your energies and abilities will rise and fall with its pattern. When it is above the centre line, go for it, when it is below, you should be resting.

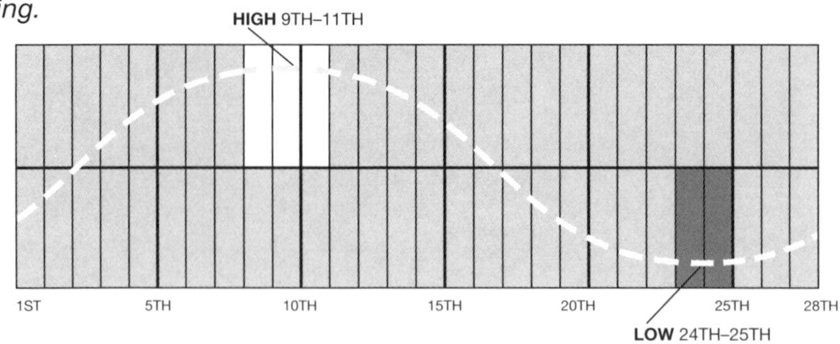

1 THURSDAY *Moon Age Day 16 Moon Sign Leo*

This is a time when you should be as open as possible and a period during which you might have to explain yourself fully to those around you. Colleagues in particular could be difficult to deal with, but only if you insist on having all your own way. Make sure you co-operate in challenging tasks.

2 FRIDAY *Moon Age Day 17 Moon Sign Virgo*

It looks as though you will now have good ideas for improving work routines and you may be able to present alternative suggestions that will make colleagues and superiors sit up and think. Beware the possibility of inspiring envy or jealousy in others and make it plain that what you now know is partly down to their experience and advice.

3 SATURDAY *Moon Age Day 18 Moon Sign Virgo*

If there are important decisions to be made you must be willing to co-operate with family members, especially with your partner. Your view ahead is becoming a little less clear than would normally be the case and with a few stumbling blocks around you need to somewhat critical of your own opinions.

4 SUNDAY *Moon Age Day 19 Moon Sign Libra*

A new sense of mission is evident but don't allow this to cause a rift between yourself and colleagues or friends. There is a slight chance that you fail to listen to the opinions of people who are important to your life and that could be a mistake. At every turn, be aware of the undertones in relationships.

5 MONDAY *Moon Age Day 20 Moon Sign Libra*

You know very well how to relate to people on their own level and it is this chameleon quality of Sagittarius that helps you to get on so well in your life. Socially speaking you should be on top form and will be the life and soul of any party that is taking place in your vicinity. One particular person will be very impressed with you.

6 TUESDAY *Moon Age Day 21 Moon Sign Libra*

You may now have especially good ideas for new business ventures and should be forging ahead in a number of different ways. The only slight fly in the ointment is that you don't stay still long enough for others to catch up with your thinking or actions. Some people need time to get used to change – but not the ever-busy Archer.

7 WEDNESDAY *Moon Age Day 22 Moon Sign Scorpio*

Your intelligence, curiosity and desire to understand everything conspire to make this a very enjoyable period. Make certain others know how you feel about things, although this should not be difficult because you communicate your feelings very well. Colleagues are likely to place ever-greater trust in you.

8 THURSDAY *Moon Age Day 23 Moon Sign Scorpio*

Opportunities could become available for profitable investment and you will be making purchases at the moment that can have a very positive bearing on your life in the days to come. You also possess a great ability to make something out of nothing, a trend that won't be lost on some of the influential people who surround you now.

9 FRIDAY *Moon Age Day 24 Moon Sign Sagittarius*

Focus all your efforts today in order to make certain you use the lunar high to your advantage. People listen to what you have to say and your words are interesting and even inspirational. You could be luckier than usual and won't have any difficulty at all seeing through a few complications in order to view your real objectives.

10 SATURDAY *Moon Age Day 25 Moon Sign Sagittarius*

You won't miss a trick when it comes to getting your own way – though you do so with such charm and eloquence that you could persuade anybody that black is white. Get onside with those you know are on a winning streak and give yourself fully to projects that have been waiting for an inspirational moment such as this.

11 SUNDAY *Moon Age Day 26 Moon Sign Sagittarius*

Be sure to remain diplomatic when you are dealing with people who can be difficult to understand. Under present trends you will also be striving for perfection, especially in terms of the way you look. When you have to learn something new be sure to take your time and to listen as carefully as you can to whoever is teaching you.

12 MONDAY *Moon Age Day 27 Moon Sign Capricorn*

With energy to spare you tackle any potential problem head on and won't be inclined to sit around at all on this particular Monday. You can be a great inspiration to others and especially so in the case of younger people. Make sure that whatever you have to impart to them is the very best of what you have learned over the years.

13 TUESDAY *Moon Age Day 28 Moon Sign Capricorn*

At work you are likely to be on top form and it won't be at all hard to impress colleagues. You have a positive bearing on those around you and will be especially good at explaining things to younger family members. In a way it doesn't matter what age you are because you are always so young at heart.

14 WEDNESDAY *Moon Age Day 29 Moon Sign Aquarius*

You now have a very good insight into the way others are likely to behave under any given circumstance. This would be another really good time to reach out and help others, particularly in the case of younger family members. Friends will allow you to have your own way when it comes to common decisions and that always makes you happy.

15 THURSDAY *Moon Age Day 0 Moon Sign Aquarius*

It is your creative potential that really shines out right now. You may not be painting a picture or making a sculpture but you are modelling life itself, which can be just as impressive. You feel the need to make your surroundings as comfortable and secure as you can, and this mood strengthens over the next couple of days at least.

16 FRIDAY *Moon Age Day 1 Moon Sign Aquarius*

Rely heavily on what colleagues and friends have to say to you. There is information about now that can be of use to you but if you don't keep your ears open you will almost certainly miss it. Current affairs will also keep you occupied, as will spending time on the telephone or your computer. Keep busy today.

17 SATURDAY *Moon Age Day 2 Moon Sign Pisces*

The Archer is much more courageous than it thinks and you prove this today by stepping in to defend someone you consider is being wronged. This outspoken attitude is what gets you noticed and people think of you as an honourable and truthful friend. Try to get your own way today without making any undue enemies.

18 SUNDAY *Moon Age Day 3 Moon Sign Pisces*

You are socially adept and able to mix with just about anyone so don't be surprised if your popularity turns out to be especially high. Of course there are always going to be people you don't like and who are not fond of you. Try as you may you can't be everyone's cup of tea – that's just the way life is so accept it.

19 MONDAY *Moon Age Day 4 Moon Sign Aries*

It is towards your career and professional matters generally that your mind is inclined to turn at the start of this particular week. There are gains on the way as a result of actions you took some time ago and romance should be going especially well for most sons and daughters of Sagittarius. New contacts prove to be very important later.

20 TUESDAY *Moon Age Day 5 Moon Sign Aries*

A warm and contented sort of day seems to be on the cards. There isn't that much you presently want from life and most of your joy comes from being willing to make others happy. As you do so, your own sense of contentment increases too. Family moments can be fun and may also bring nostalgic periods.

21 WEDNESDAY *Moon Age Day 6 Moon Sign Taurus*

There are gains to be made on the financial front today, mostly from putting yourself in the best possible position at the most advantageous time. Don't get too hung up on details at work and take the longer-term view whenever possible. Romance is also on the up and new relationships could be in the offing for some Archers now.

22 THURSDAY *Moon Age Day 7 Moon Sign Taurus*

Stop and look before you take a chance today because your enthusiasm will sometimes be greater than your capabilities. There are times when it might be best to enlist the support of someone who is an expert in their particular field. Once you have their advice you will be able to get ahead that much better.

23 FRIDAY *Moon Age Day 8 Moon Sign Taurus*

Keep up your efforts to get ahead and plan now for the forthcoming weekend. Almost anyone you meet today could be that person who has the key to success you are looking for. What really sets you apart is your enthusiasm and your zest for life. Other people notice it and want a slice of the action. Socially speaking life should be fine.

24 SATURDAY *Moon Age Day 9 Moon Sign Gemini*

This is not likely to be a straightforward time. There could be hitches and complications to deal with and the lunar low may leave you feeling as though you are not fully in charge. However, as long as you are willing to accept advice and support from others you should maintain a degree of control and some contentment.

25 SUNDAY

Moon Age Day 10 Moon Sign Gemini

Any really important decisions should probably be left until later. It isn't that you are likely to make any major blunders but neither are you fully in command of your life in the way that you prefer. Be careful with money and don't sign any important documents until tomorrow at the earliest. Your partner should show strong support.

26 MONDAY

Moon Age Day 11 Moon Sign Cancer

If you look back across the last few weeks you will probably see how much further you have come than you expected. Standard responses are not enough today because you need to add to your successes by being extraordinary. Anything that makes you stand out in a crowd is grist to the mill and helps you achieve so much more.

27 TUESDAY

Moon Age Day 12 Moon Sign Cancer

Although it might seem that life is hard going in one way or another, you are still making progress, no matter how slow. That is what matters for Sagittarius and you only need to regroup when things have stopped altogether. Just when you think you have reached a full stop, another sentence begins.

28 WEDNESDAY

Moon Age Day 13 Moon Sign Leo

Your capacity for sound judgement now strengthens and since others recognise this instinctively, they too will be coming to you for help and advice. That's fine as far as it goes but you cannot live their lives for them and in the end you need to help people to make their own decisions. Look out for a romantic fling.

March

2018

Your Month at a Glance

+ = Opportunities are around — = Be on the defensive = Life is pretty ordinary

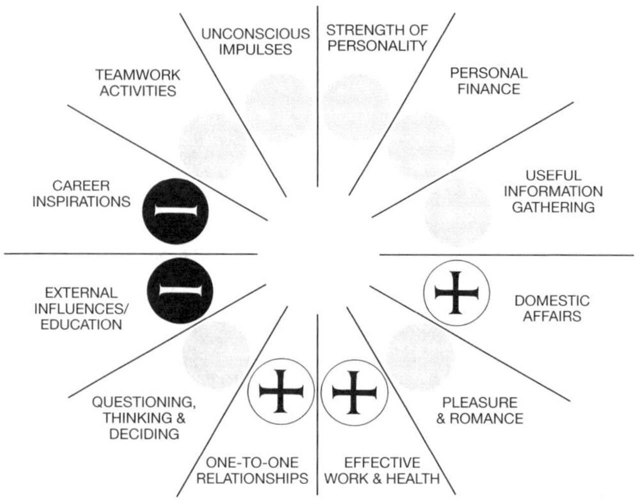

March Highs and Lows

Here I show you how the rhythms of the Moon will affect you this month. Like the tide, your energies and abilities will rise and fall with its pattern. When it is above the centre line, go for it, when it is below, you should be resting.

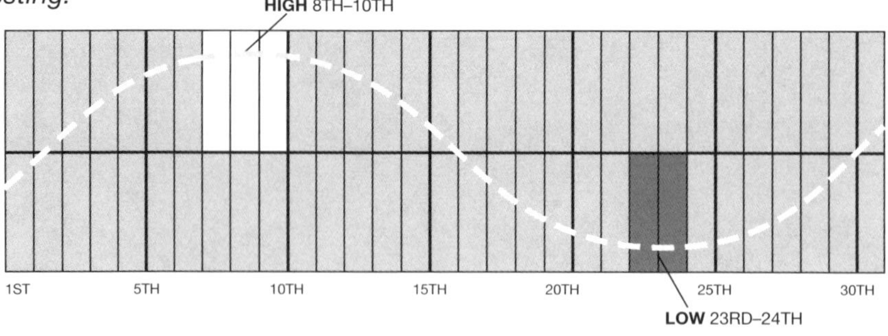

1 THURSDAY

Moon Age Day 14 Moon Sign Leo

The start of a new month also brings the promise of spring, a time of year that is likely to be good for you. Take some time out right now to monitor how things are changing in the world beyond your door. These alterations in nature are matched by subtle changes taking place within your own personality. Winter is over for you.

2 FRIDAY

Moon Age Day 15 Moon Sign Virgo

You should be in a get-up-and-go sort of mood, at least during the first part of today and you will actively want to get on well with anyone who you see as being of use to you. This might sound selfish but in the end you will make certain that others share in any successes you have. The Archer is always a team player but especially so now.

3 SATURDAY

Moon Age Day 16 Moon Sign Virgo

Career matters seem to be your chief concern under present trends. Those Archers who are presently involved in full-time education might be the luckiest of all, as it appears that you absorb new facts and figures like a sponge. Most impressively, you can proceed along rocky paths without stumbling once.

4 SUNDAY

Moon Age Day 17 Moon Sign Libra

Teamwork and events taking place in groups begin to take up more of your time and it looks as though you are now fully in control of one or two wayward planets. You will be less dominant in your speech and very likely to play a diplomatic role. This is the Archer that everyone knows and loves.

5 MONDAY

Moon Age Day 18 Moon Sign Libra

Your commanding personality is definitely on display when it comes to professional matters and this would be a good time to make sure everyone knows exactly what you want to do to get on in life. The more you explain yourself, the less you will be inclined to struggle later. Romance begins to take a central role.

6 TUESDAY

Moon Age Day 19 Moon Sign Scorpio

Things should remain generally progressive and although there are situations you won't want to address today, what you do take on is undertaken with confidence and a smile. In a personal sense you should be happy enough and you might even discover that one particular person is making a play for you in a very original way.

7 WEDNESDAY *Moon Age Day 20 Moon Sign Scorpio*

Your ability to get along with others sets you apart and you can definitely use this skill to your best advantage right now. At home you will be happy to spend time talking to those you love and your partner can be the source of great joy, even without realising that they are doing anything different.

8 THURSDAY *Moon Age Day 21 Moon Sign Sagittarius*

You should feel confident and self-assured today, which is part of the gift offered by the lunar high. Things that worried or irritated you across the last few days will now take a more realistic place in your mind and you have what it takes to make people notice you in a very positive way. You might even be pushing your luck today.

9 FRIDAY *Moon Age Day 22 Moon Sign Sagittarius*

The way you can motivate others at this time will be a joy to behold. Although you are likely to do yourself a great deal of good your greatest claim to fame today is the way you do so much for other people. Some of this is just a natural consequence of being an Archer but a few of your actions are pure gold.

10 SATURDAY *Moon Age Day 23 Moon Sign Sagittarius*

Your social life is extremely important at the moment and you will sacrifice almost anything in order to have a good time with your friends. As a result a few responsibilities might be left hanging, for which you might kick yourself later. Prioritise well and perhaps you can have the best of both worlds.

11 SUNDAY *Moon Age Day 24 Moon Sign Capricorn*

Look out for some minor confusion today and don't get too deeply involved in situations you know from the start are going to become complicated. You may end up being given jobs you simply cannot undertake and if this is the case, speak out straight away. Today it is vital for you to tell people how you really feel.

12 MONDAY *Moon Age Day 25 Moon Sign Capricorn*

The pace of life is still fast and you should be able to make use of every little opportunity that comes your way. Socially you should be happy to take centre stage and it would take someone extremely bright and fascinating to steal your limelight. Look after your money and avoid taking chances unless you are sure of yourself.

13 TUESDAY *Moon Age Day 26 Moon Sign Aquarius*

The challenge today could lie in keeping one step ahead of competitors. This will not necessarily be a professional matter because it could also relate to sport or any other sphere of your always-busy life. Although you always want to win you are probably keener to do so under present trends and might occasionally go too far.

14 WEDNESDAY *Moon Age Day 27 Moon Sign Aquarius*

Now you seem to have an opinion about everything and this could get slightly wearing for the people with whom you spend most of your time. The trouble is that what you believe today might not be the same as yesterday and that can sometimes make it difficult for others to keep up. Try for a little consistency if possible.

15 THURSDAY *Moon Age Day 28 Moon Sign Aquarius*

When it comes to practical issues you now want to roll up your sleeves and get on with things. Not everyone is likely to be in the same frame of mind so make sure that you don't end up carrying others. Before you embark on anything make sure that those around you are as motivated as you are.

16 FRIDAY *Moon Age Day 29 Moon Sign Pisces*

This is another good time to improve your prospects and to show exactly what you are made of. Life is very good for you at this time and increases your potential for getting ahead of rivals and showing your true colours. Naturally, not everyone will be on your side but the people who matter most probably will be.

17 SATURDAY new moon *Moon Age Day 0 Moon Sign Pisces*

Take every opportunity for financial gain while the present trends last. You will know instinctively how to behave with your money, which certainly isn't always the case for the average Archer. At the same time be careful to save a little because unexpected cash all too often burns a hole in your pocket.

18 SUNDAY *Moon Age Day 1 Moon Sign Aries*

Along with a very sharp mind comes a fairly sharp tongue. Not everything you say is going to go down well with either colleagues or friends and you might get yourself into some sort of trouble with relatives. It is so often the case that Sagittarians engage their mouth before their brain is fully in gear.

19 MONDAY

Moon Age Day 2 Moon Sign Aries

Now is a good time for professional success and you really do need to keep your foot down this week, whilst the prospects are so good. Of course you will have to spend some time thinking about your actions but in the main you are happier when you are doing things and thinking on the way. Romance is also on the cards.

OSTARA.

20 TUESDAY

Moon Age Day 3 Moon Sign Aries

You can now reap the benefits of a good and successful social life. Here you may find that you are more successful than you are at work, though in the end it's the same thing because you have what it takes to mix business with pleasure. Despite some offhand remarks on your part you remain essentially popular.

21 WEDNESDAY

Moon Age Day 4 Moon Sign Taurus

Take time to sort things out and to look at matters objectively. You are inclined to rush into situations, hoping that things will turn out right and that you will be able to extricate yourself if situations turn sour. This isn't always the case but if you analyse everything carefully, all should be well.

22 THURSDAY

Moon Age Day 5 Moon Sign Taurus

There is rarely a better time than this for expressing yourself. You should be well up-to-date with necessary tasks at this part of the week and you should be more than half way through something you probably thought would take much longer than it has. Things seem to be falling into place nicely for you.

23 FRIDAY ☿

Moon Age Day 6 Moon Sign Gemini

Some of your desires are likely to go unfulfilled today but there will always be options, even with the lunar low around. Rely on the help of those around you more than you might normally do and be prepared to change direction if necessary. Deal with all communications by post and email whilst things are generally quiet.

24 SATURDAY ☿

Moon Age Day 7 Moon Sign Gemini

The second day of the lunar low coincides with a Saturday this month and it is possible that if you have already decided to rest and relax a little that you won't even notice it. It is only when you pit yourself against insurmountable odds that you will get tired and perhaps slightly depressed. Friendship is the most important rock of all at this time.

25 SUNDAY ☿ *Moon Age Day 8 Moon Sign Cancer*

You are now quite self-motivated and you don't need encouragement from anyone else in order to get on with anything. Actually you might have to slow down in order to wait for others to catch up and this won't please you at all. As the day gets older you may be slightly less fractious with yourself and others.

26 MONDAY ☿ *Moon Age Day 9 Moon Sign Cancer*

This is a time during which you can expand your sense of social belonging. For one reason or another you have been more isolated this month than is strictly good for a Sagittarian. Now things are falling into place in such a way that you can really pull with the rest of the team. Your involvement in projects would be appreciated.

27 TUESDAY ☿ *Moon Age Day 10 Moon Sign Leo*

This could be a very good day for thinking about new job prospects. Things have been a little up and down this month but you have rarely failed to impress the right people at the right time. You might be considered for more responsibility or you could even be thinking about exploring a totally new direction.

28 WEDNESDAY ☿ *Moon Age Day 11 Moon Sign Leo*

Today is probably the best time for membership in clubs, groups and organisations of one sort or another. You will have what it takes to rise up the ranks quickly and you could also be sorting out a reorganisation that will also stand you in good stead. Beware of being accused of finding ways to feather your own nest, though.

29 THURSDAY ☿ *Moon Age Day 12 Moon Sign Virgo*

Friendship remains of critical importance today because it doesn't matter how well you are getting on across the board, you need genuine companionship if you are going to feel really good about yourself. Today brings you a little closer to understanding your own motivations regarding a confusing situation.

30 FRIDAY ☿ *Moon Age Day 13 Moon Sign Virgo*

This is a great time to be doing things at a group level. By getting together with others you have the benefit of a different point of view, to add to your own considerations. You think very quickly and not everyone else does. This means you need to have patience and to be very specific when it comes to showing you are listening.

Full moon

31 SATURDAY ☿

Moon Age Day 14 Moon Sign Libra

Love can play an important role in your life this weekend. Find time to tell someone how important they are to you and, if possible, spoil them rotten. You will be amazed what a difference this will make later on and just how much good you can do yourself and them. Finding the right words is never difficult for the Archer.

April

2018

Your Month at a Glance

(+) = Opportunities are around (–) = Be on the defensive ( ) = Life is pretty ordinary

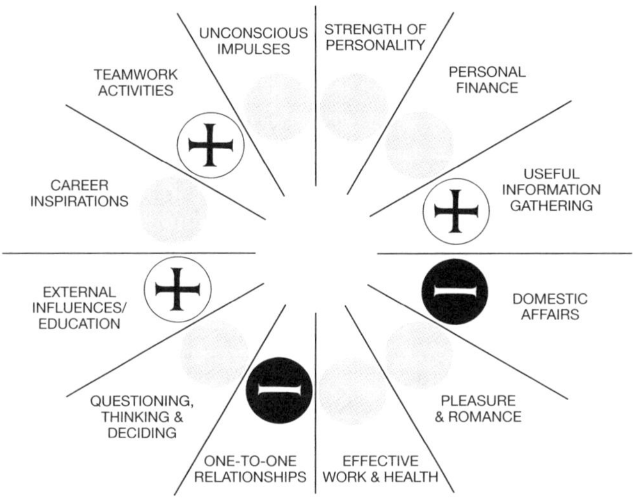

April Highs and Lows

Here I show you how the rhythms of the Moon will affect you this month. Like the tide, your energies and abilities will rise and fall with its pattern. When it is above the centre line, go for it, when it is below, you should be resting.

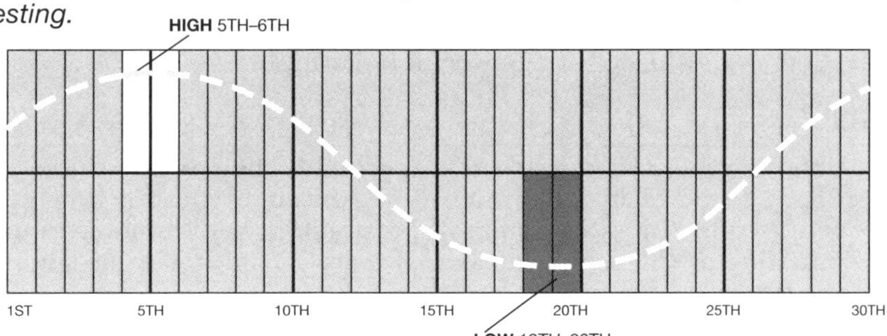

1 SUNDAY ☿ *Moon Age Day 15 Moon Sign Libra*

A partner in your life could offer compelling reasons for a change in direction and you would be well advised to look at what is on offer without dismissing it out of hand. A sudden shift in routines is possible at work and in almost every sense there is something slightly disturbing but at the same time exciting about today.

2 MONDAY ☿ *Moon Age Day 16 Moon Sign Scorpio*

Variety is the spice of life as far as you are concerned and you will be doing everything you can to make situations more exciting. Not everyone will be on your wavelength at present but those who are know exactly what makes you tick and how to please you. As for the others – just ignore them for now.

3 TUESDAY ☿ *Moon Age Day 17 Moon Sign Scorpio*

You have a great drive to succeed and may be slightly more focused on what needs doing in a practical sense if you are to get ahead. Finishing something at work could prove to be lucrative and you definitely do need to rule a line under some of your past efforts. When it comes to getting on with others you should have no problems today.

4 WEDNESDAY ☿ *Moon Age Day 18 Moon Sign Scorpio*

Where others are concerned you remain eager to please and quite willing to go that extra step in order to enchant those you love. Romance is higher on your agenda than it has been in recent days and you will find the right words to make that most special person feel even more loved. Avoid pointless domestic routines today.

5 THURSDAY ☿ *Moon Age Day 19 Moon Sign Sagittarius*

There is a great desire within you now to get involved in anything new and you have the resilience to take on a whole host of new possibilities until you decide what is going to be your thing for the future. Whatever your accomplishments may be, they are more emphasised under the protection and influence of a powerful lunar high.

6 FRIDAY ☿ *Moon Age Day 20 Moon Sign Sagittarius*

It is time to get new projects off the ground, though now these are more likely to be related to your work. Although you can become a little confused by the sheer weight of possibilities, you should get more discriminating as the day progresses. Beware a tendency to be slightly pushy at times.

7 SATURDAY ☿ *Moon Age Day 21 Moon Sign Capricorn*

Encounters with a friend could prove to be inspirational and it appears that you will be on your best behaviour today – which let's face it isn't always the case for the Archer. Nothing will stop you being mischievous because that's the way nature made you but your sense of humour isn't quite as peculiar today as it sometimes is.

8 SUNDAY ☿ *Moon Age Day 22 Moon Sign Capricorn*

Getting the very most out of social encounters with friends should be quite easy, though there is something a little quiet about you whilst the Moon occupies its present position. At work you will probably have to think on your feet because you could be lacking some important piece of information. Stay cool and focused.

9 MONDAY ☿ *Moon Age Day 23 Moon Sign Capricorn*

You are clearly impatient now to get things going the way you would wish but a little patience goes a long way and the result of your efforts will be that much better if you remain circumspect. Sometimes your mind is like a badly organised workbasket but it is what comes out of it that counts and for you at the moment that's pure gold.

10 TUESDAY ☿ *Moon Age Day 24 Moon Sign Aquarius*

The need for familiarity and reassurance from the people you love is very strong under present planetary trends. You might even be feeling slightly unsettled or nervous, though without really knowing why. Just rely on the good offices of people who have never let you down in the past because they are unlikely to do so now.

11 WEDNESDAY ☿ *Moon Age Day 25 Moon Sign Aquarius*

A reflective mood prevails today and you are going deeper within yourself under present trends than would normally be the case. This makes you more analytical – especially of your own past actions. You can't change what has happened but you may be able to sort things out better for the future. Avoid irksome or noisy people for the moment.

12 THURSDAY ☿ *Moon Age Day 26 Moon Sign Pisces*

Your expectations can be too high on occasions but it looks as though you will be quite realistic between now and the weekend. This means a steady sort of day and plenty of chance to make others happy. It is the little things you do that could be so important and which make you more popular than ever.

13 FRIDAY ☿ *Moon Age Day 27 Moon Sign Pisces*

You may enjoy a much-improved romantic life at this time and part of the reason for this is that you have more time to tell people how you feel. Finding the right words isn't difficult for the Archer but stopping still long enough to express them can be a problem. People will be pleased if you take time to chat.

14 SATURDAY ☿ *Moon Age Day 28 Moon Sign Pisces*

There are moments today when it would be interesting and rewarding to sit and think. Thinking is a process that usually takes place for Sagittarians at the same time as taking action. However there are occasions when a little prior planning can be worth a great deal. This is especially true today.

15 SUNDAY *Moon Age Day 29 Moon Sign Aries*

A matter involving communication may run into some trouble today if you get hold of the wrong end of the stick. If you are in any doubt at all it would be worthwhile making sure that you understand what people really mean. Don't be too keen to sign documents or to make long-term financial commitments for the next day or two.

16 MONDAY *Moon Age Day 0 Moon Sign Aries*

Your spirits should be high at the beginning of this working week and it looks as though you will find it easy enough to get ahead of the herd. With plenty to play for and a generally positive attitude there is very little that will fail to fall into your lap. The one area of life that may need attention is a slightly flagging romance.

17 TUESDAY *Moon Age Day 1 Moon Sign Taurus*

Now you can renew your efforts and succeed in ways that were not open to you only a few days ago. There will probably be new opportunities coming along at work, while at home you are in the mood for making yourself more comfortable in some way. This is likely to be a busy day of rapid progress.

18 WEDNESDAY *Moon Age Day 2 Moon Sign Taurus*

You may now be inclined to fall behind others in some way and will be frantically doing everything you can to prove yourself to colleagues and superiors. There really is no need because people don't judge you on one day's activity. The impression you have made of late isn't lost on the people who count.

19 THURSDAY

Moon Age Day 3 Moon Sign Gemini

On this particular day you are hardly likely to be filled with either enthusiasm or your usual energy. You might have to rely on what others can do for you and you should listen to good advice, no matter where it comes from. There is something quite unusual about your thought processes just now but you will be very intuitive.

20 FRIDAY

Moon Age Day 4 Moon Sign Gemini

Close companions could cause you to think more deeply and this is all part of the process brought about by the Moon in your opposite sign. Don't bottle up minor frustrations but be willing to talk about them – probably to almost anyone who will listen. A friend may have particular needs of you now, even though they could irritate you.

21 SATURDAY

Moon Age Day 5 Moon Sign Cancer

It may seem that there is great energy around today – though in reality you are simply being your normal self. Your cheerful and optimistic approach to life has a profound influence on those around you and it looks as though people will put themselves out on your behalf. A good time to ask for favours.

22 SUNDAY

Moon Age Day 6 Moon Sign Cancer

When it comes to the social side of life you won't need many invitations in order to get involved. You love to be around people who are happy and forward-looking and should willingly get involved in new possibilities at the moment. Keep an eye open for advantages that come from people living far away or working at a distance.

23 MONDAY

Moon Age Day 7 Moon Sign Leo

It is towards money that your mind has turned on a number of occasions during April and today is no exception. You want to make certain that you will be as comfortable as you would wish in the long-term future and show a great ability to be inventive when planning ahead. At home you may need extra patience today.

24 TUESDAY

Moon Age Day 8 Moon Sign Leo

Getting to grips with disputes that are taking place in your family or friendship circle could prove to be a real nuisance on a day when you need all your energy to focus on getting ahead in a practical sense. If you can't make others see eye-to-eye, in the end just leave them to get on with it.

25 WEDNESDAY *Moon Age Day 9 Moon Sign Virgo*

Outwardly you appear very calm, even on those occasions when you are very nervous inside. This ability is especially enhanced at present and you will often appear to be far more confident than is actually the case. Since you can fool almost anyone, get on and show just how unflappable you seem to be.

26 THURSDAY *Moon Age Day 10 Moon Sign Virgo*

The small details of life won't matter at all today because you are pushing forward on all fronts and won't be diverted by irrelevant details. Not only are you able to achieve things for yourself but you are also sticking up for those who don't have quite the level of drive that comes as second nature to you. Look out for new starts in relationships.

27 FRIDAY *Moon Age Day 11 Moon Sign Virgo*

Loving relationships now prove to be highly rewarding and this is likely to be the area of life that interests you the most between now and the weekend. Concerns regarding work will be put on hold because you can't concentrate on everything at the same time. New personalities begin to have a significant bearing on your life.

28 SATURDAY *Moon Age Day 12 Moon Sign Libra*

You might not be at work this weekend but this will not prevent you from getting on famously in almost anything you decide to undertake. They say a change is as good as a rest and that certainly seems to be the case as far as you are concerned. Amongst your many interests today, find time for family members.

29 SUNDAY *Moon Age Day 13 Moon Sign Libra*

You are somehow less practical at the moment, perhaps because your mind is presently so creative. That means that certain things probably won't get done, or else they will take much longer than usual. It might be best to avoid routines and to go off on a trip or a shopping spree with people you like.

30 MONDAY *Moon Age Day 14 Moon Sign Scorpio*

Something may seem to be missing today and that is probably because other people are not doing what is expected of them. Give a little nudge if necessary but don't push things too much. In the end you may decide that it is simply easier to get on and do things on your own. Someone you don't see too often may make an appearance later.

May

2018

Your Month at a Glance

(+) = Opportunities are around (−) = Be on the defensive ( ) = Life is pretty ordinary

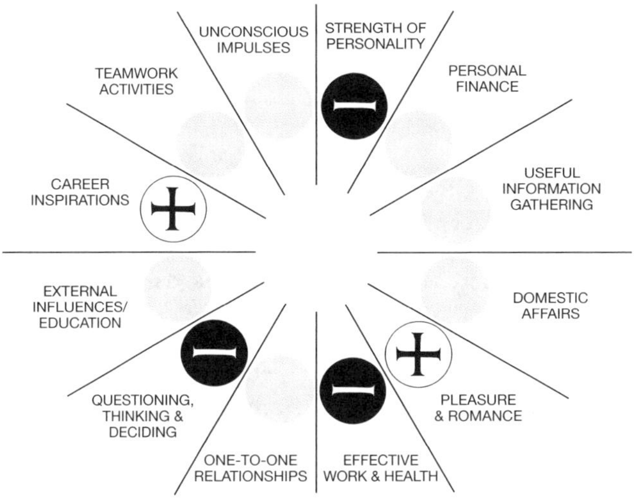

May Highs and Lows

Here I show you how the rhythms of the Moon will affect you this month. Like the tide, your energies and abilities will rise and fall with its pattern. When it is above the centre line, go for it, when it is below, you should be resting.

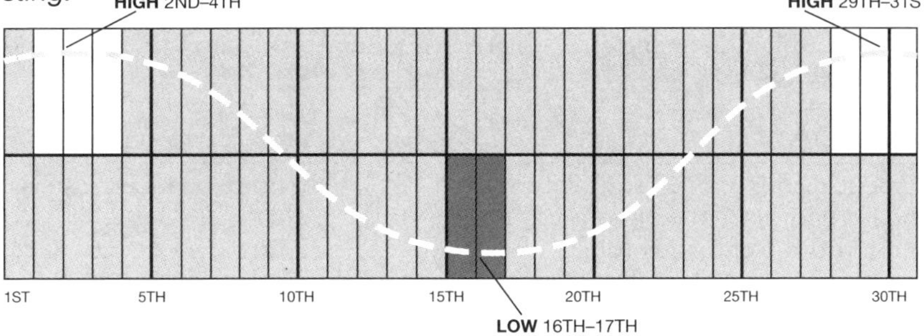

1 TUESDAY *Moon Age Day 15 Moon Sign Scorpio*

Don't expect to make too much headway in the big world beyond your door because that comes later. It is the details of life that seem to interest you the most for the moment and you will be busy planning your actions for other times. Not much seems to be achieved but in reality you are sowing the seeds of much success later.

2 WEDNESDAY *Moon Age Day 16 Moon Sign Sagittarius*

You are very much on the ball and anxious to do whatever is possible to make things happen. If there is any problem today it could come from the direction of people who seem to constantly slow you down and who will not modify their own stance to accommodate yours. Perhaps you are expecting too much of them?

3 THURSDAY *Moon Age Day 17 Moon Sign Sagittarius*

It should not be difficult to get your message across to others today. You are filled with enterprise and determination but at the same time you are very sensitive to what those close to you might think about your actions. That is why you will actively seek co-operation rather than competition today.

4 FRIDAY *Moon Age Day 18 Moon Sign Sagittarius*

Keep life as varied as you can but without pushing yourself too hard or taking on more than you can reasonably deal with. At work you can be one jump ahead of the competition without really trying and it is also possible that you will be planning for journeys you intend to undertake in the summer months.

5 SATURDAY *Moon Age Day 19 Moon Sign Capricorn*

Beware of giving free advice to others because if you do there could be a price to pay later. Let people decide things for themselves, whilst you simply prod or gently push them in certain directions. There is a fine line between assisting and influencing and this is something you have to learn under present trends.

6 SUNDAY *Moon Age Day 20 Moon Sign Capricorn*

Current trends should stimulate you to take a few more chances, especially when it comes to making money. However, there are times when the Archer is just too adventurous for its own good so some care is necessary. Get in touch with people you don't see often, especially those living far away.

7 MONDAY *Moon Age Day 21 Moon Sign Aquarius*

Disputes are more likely today but will probably restrict themselves to the outside world. For example, you are unlikely to have that much patience with pointless or silly rules and political correctness will be very frustrating. You can't stand being told what to do and especially not by those you do not respect.

8 TUESDAY *Moon Age Day 22 Moon Sign Aquarius*

Although you continue to communicate well with others there may be occasions today when you fail to understand exactly what is required of you. If you don't know what to do, the only way forward is to ask and then ask again if necessary. Friends should be warm and supportive, especially by the time the evening arrives.

9 WEDNESDAY *Moon Age Day 23 Moon Sign Aquarius*

While your career might have plenty going for it, you are looking beyond the immediate and thinking about things that are a long way into the future. Most of the excitement in your life is potential at the moment but all that is likely to change in a very short while. Plan now for a weekend that offers diversity and fun.

10 THURSDAY *Moon Age Day 24 Moon Sign Pisces*

Your greatest sense of security right now comes from those elements of life you know and understand. It is likely that you will be less adventurous than is usually the case but you will have time to think about family members and to support your friends. People who are having problems will gravitate towards you under present trends.

11 FRIDAY *Moon Age Day 25 Moon Sign Pisces*

A day of minor short-term increases can be expected on the money front and you may also be in a good position to look ahead and plan some sort of coup for the future. Avoid getting involved in pointless disputes – not because you would lose any argument but rather on account of your present temper, which can be quite strong.

12 SATURDAY *Moon Age Day 26 Moon Sign Aries*

Now comes the time to let go of whatever has been occupying you. The last constraint is out of the way and you move forward with a speed of a bullet. Not everyone will be prepared for this sudden burst of activity so you need to allow people time to catch up. New friends are possible at this time and you may meet old pals again.

13 SUNDAY *Moon Age Day 27 Moon Sign Aries*

A focus on money shows a great potential for profit around this time. Business deals are dealt with easily and you also have a strong interest in subjects that have not played a part in your thinking before. Newer and better ways of doing things that have stayed the same for years are now on the way but be aware that not everyone will be happy.

14 MONDAY *Moon Age Day 28 Moon Sign Taurus*

Certain people will respond to you right now and these are the sorts of individuals you will mix with by choice. Avoid getting yourself into a pickle by acting on impulse and try to think things through if at all possible. In particular you need to be careful not to say or do the wrong thing.

15 TUESDAY *Moon Age Day 0 Moon Sign Taurus*

There is no doubting your bravery around this time but they do say that fools rush in where angels fear to tread. Sagittarius is instinctively courageous but you must give some thought to your actions – ahead of them and not after. Minor accidents are a possibility, as are embarrassing gaffes unless you think before you speak.

16 WEDNESDAY *Moon Age Day 1 Moon Sign Gemini*

Daily circumstances come and go but you remain insulated from most of them. For some this means being locked inside their own thoughts, which is almost totally alien to the Archer's nature. Friends will have the power to bring you out of yourself and it would be sensible today to spend a few hours in their company if you can.

17 THURSDAY *Moon Age Day 2 Moon Sign Gemini*

The Moon is in your opposite sign and the lunar low is with you at this time. Once again you withdraw into yourself more than is normally the case, making it difficult for those around you to understand the seesaw nature you are presently displaying. It's time to explain yourself, especially to your partner.

18 FRIDAY *Moon Age Day 3 Moon Sign Cancer*

It is possible for you to create an atmosphere of tension around yourself today, even though you have no real intention of doing so. It is probably your excitable nature that is to blame, together with your determination to keep people guessing about your intended actions. Maybe you should come clean earlier and avoid problems.

19 SATURDAY *Moon Age Day 4 Moon Sign Cancer*

It is towards the strictly practical that your mind is apt to turn under prevailing astrological trends and if there is anything you have been meaning to do in or around your home, now is the time to get cracking. You won't run short of energy but it is possible that you will need to call on the expertise of someone in the know.

20 SUNDAY *Moon Age Day 5 Moon Sign Leo*

Avoid making rash purchases at the moment and when it comes to doing deals of any sort, be absolutely sure before you commit yourself. You might not be quite as astute as usual and your tendency to rush in and act instantly might not be such a blessing in certain circumstances.

21 MONDAY *Moon Age Day 6 Moon Sign Leo*

Communication becomes easier and easier in this new working week and the influence you have over others is likely to be much stronger. At some time during today you may recognise a much quieter side to your nature and this could predominate during the evening and through the first part of tomorrow.

22 TUESDAY *Moon Age Day 7 Moon Sign Leo*

Get to know people better now and especially those individuals who have it in their power to be of special use to you. Don't get on the wrong side of superiors, even when you feel that what they are saying and doing might be wrong. What matters most of all if you want to feather your own nest today is diplomacy.

23 WEDNESDAY *Moon Age Day 8 Moon Sign Virgo*

It's time to talk to someone who really knows their business. In a particularly demanding situation you can struggle on and might well win through in the end. On the other hand if you are willing to seek out the right person you can get a task out of the way in a fraction of the time, leaving you free for other things.

24 THURSDAY *Moon Age Day 9 Moon Sign Virgo*

Not all opinions you hear at the moment seem to be equally valid. On the contrary you are inclined to dismiss loud or insensitive types out of hand. As you favour the underdog right now and show yourself to be very courageous when dealing with bosses, or people you think are ignorant, you gain respect.

25 FRIDAY *Moon Age Day 10 Moon Sign Libra*

Under certain circumstances you might feel like withdrawing into yourself, mainly because you don't always understand what is going on around you. Try to avoid this tendency because no zodiac sign learns more quickly by practical experience than yours does. Romantically speaking you should be on top form.

26 SATURDAY *Moon Age Day 11 Moon Sign Libra*

The first part of the weekend carries more domestic issues and necessities than the second, which is why a good part of Saturday might be spent sorting things out with family members. Younger people especially could be a bit of a trial and you will need to be very calm and collected if you are not to lose your temper with someone.

27 SUNDAY *Moon Age Day 12 Moon Sign Scorpio*

It might seem as though not everyone has your best interests at heart today but you do need to look at the situation carefully. It is possible that someone is simply watching out for you and doesn't want you to make a great mistake. Thinking again about any decision you want to take would be no bad thing under present trends.

28 MONDAY *Moon Age Day 13 Moon Sign Scorpio*

It appears that you are spending more of today thinking and rather less taking any sort of action. That's not surprising because the Moon is passing through your solar twelfth house. This can put you into a sort of pleasant daze but it doesn't prevent you from thinking about what you intend to do in only a few hours.

29 TUESDAY *Moon Age Day 14 Moon Sign Sagittarius*

Everything should come together for you today and the monthly visit of the Moon to your own zodiac sign will put you into a really good frame of mind. While others are planning what they might do, you are putting your schemes into positive action. The Archer can certainly turn a few heads under present astrological trends.

30 WEDNESDAY *Moon Age Day 15 Moon Sign Sagittarius*

For most Sagittarian individuals, problems should now be few and far between. You are capable, articulate, kind and attentive, and people are sure to notice you a lot. Of course that does mean being on your best behaviour but there is nothing especially difficult about that. You show special concern for family members at present.

31 THURSDAY

Moon Age Day 16 Moon Sign Sagittarius

Keep up the general pace and don't allow yourself to be thwarted by a few little problems that you can solve with hardly any thought at all. Your popularity continues to rise and there should be no lack of social opportunities for you now. Sagittarians who have been looking for love might be in their element now.

June

2018

Your Month at a Glance

(+) = Opportunities are around (–) = Be on the defensive ( ) = Life is pretty ordinary

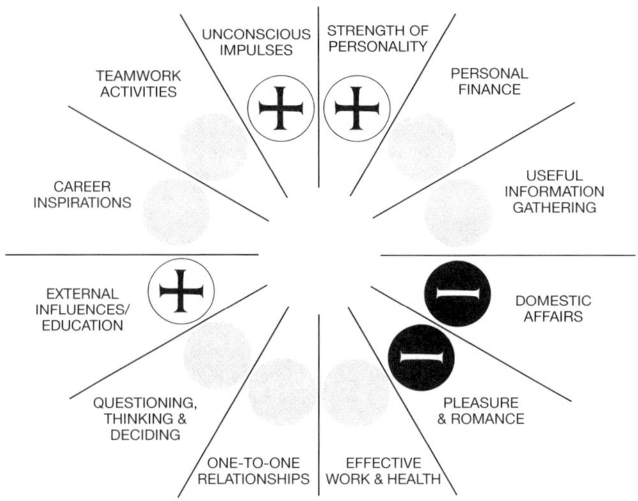

June Highs and Lows

Here I show you how the rhythms of the Moon will affect you this month. Like the tide, your energies and abilities will rise and fall with its pattern. When it is above the centre line, go for it, when it is below, you should be resting.

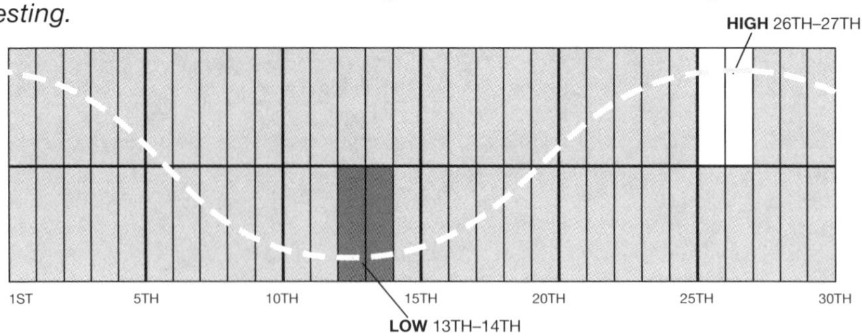

1 FRIDAY *Moon Age Day 17 Moon Sign Capricorn*

Your efforts to concentrate today could well be thwarted. The problem is that you might have too many things to think about, which is just as bad as having none. A little focus is called for, together with a better way of planning your day. Progress can still be made but only if you know what you are doing.

2 SATURDAY *Moon Age Day 18 Moon Sign Capricorn*

You can now move forward in a very significant way and whatever has held you back recently will probably be removed from the scenario. It is probable that you won't even need to intervene on some occasions because life sorts itself out. Give and take at home should be easy enough and even awkward relatives should fall into line now.

3 SUNDAY *Moon Age Day 19 Moon Sign Aquarius*

This can be a very advantageous period as far as money is concerned and you seem to be especially good at juggling your finances – thus keeping more money in your bank account and less in the hands of other people. New personalities are likely to enter your life around now and should bring with them some startling news.

4 MONDAY *Moon Age Day 20 Moon Sign Aquarius*

The pace of life begins to gain momentum – a prospect you will certainly relish. When it comes to getting your message across to others you are now in a winning position and your silver-tongued eloquence knows no bounds. Keep up your efforts to make a splash socially and find ways to use this evening to your advantage.

5 TUESDAY *Moon Age Day 21 Moon Sign Aquarius*

You may now feel more creative and expressive, especially when it comes to the romantic side of life. You will be impressive to just about anyone you encounter but nowhere will you make a bigger splash than with your partner. The Archer can be quite poetic and now is as good a time as any to write a sonnet or sing a romantic song.

6 WEDNESDAY *Moon Age Day 22 Moon Sign Pisces*

Certain matters at home could be getting rather heavy, which is why in the main you would rather avoid them for the time being. Out in the world beyond your door there are demands being made of you that you may find difficult to assess but your quick mind will go to work on these issues and make sense of them soon enough.

7 THURSDAY *Moon Age Day 23 Moon Sign Pisces*

Your home and family life might fall under the influence of someone in a position of authority. If this turns out to be the case, respond in a positive and adult way – in which case you stand to gain as a result. Don't be secretive when you really have nothing to hide at home and at work.

8 FRIDAY *Moon Age Day 24 Moon Sign Aries*

When it comes to material progress you definitely seem to be on the ball around this time. You can exploit the possibility of starting a new venture and will probably be blessed with a little more money than you might have been expecting. If some of your plans are thwarted you have what it takes to change direction quickly.

9 SATURDAY *Moon Age Day 25 Moon Sign Aries*

It looks as though some Sagittarians will be on the threshold of better times, especially when it comes to financial security. Partly as a result of what you have done in the past but also on account of your present actions, your bank balance could be increasing. You should be good company this weekend.

10 SUNDAY *Moon Age Day 26 Moon Sign Aries*

Your talent for wheeling and dealing knows no bounds but do remember that there are people out there who are just as cunning but far more devious than you can be. Don't lay anything on the line today and avoid gambling at all. If ever there was a day when even an Archer could be hoodwinked, this is surely it. Stick close to those you know.

11 MONDAY *Moon Age Day 27 Moon Sign Taurus*

Be as lively as you can at all times today. The better you show yourself in public, the more gains will be coming your way. It's likely that you will be very spontaneous and somewhat unpredictable but that won't work against your best interests because it is the way people prefer you to be.

12 TUESDAY *Moon Age Day 28 Moon Sign Taurus*

Today is favourable for all intellectual endeavours and for increasing your knowledge about the world generally. It's true that some tasks you are set will seem to take ages but what matters the most at the moment is that you do them to the best of your ability. Be a little circumspect before you spend large amount of money now.

13 WEDNESDAY *Moon Age Day 0 Moon Sign Gemini*

It might not be plain sailing all the way at work but your social and personal life is likely to remain broadly unaffected by the lunar low. This is the area of life in which you should concentrate your efforts and you can leave others to take some of the strain in a professional sense. Home and family suddenly become very important.

14 THURSDAY *Moon Age Day 1 Moon Sign Gemini*

Trends move on and now money matters and security are your major priority. You are likely to concentrate a good deal on getting things solid and dependable in your life generally. You could also have travel on your mind, though this is more likely to be in terms of planning rather than a case of packing your bags now.

15 FRIDAY *Moon Age Day 2 Moon Sign Cancer*

This is a very good time for getting yourself and everyone around you as organised as possible. You can be successful, but to do so you need to be streamlined in your approach to life and not allow woolly thinking to get in the way. Most people will be quite happy to take you at face value.

16 SATURDAY *Moon Age Day 3 Moon Sign Cancer*

Self expression seems to be the best key to happiness at the moment and you certainly won't be pleased with yourself if you sense that your message isn't getting across. Take time out to show the world how caring and kind you can be. This is especially true in the case of your partner or close family members.

17 SUNDAY *Moon Age Day 4 Moon Sign Leo*

You now seem to be slightly more contemplative and less inclined to follow your instincts without a little thought on the way. Reconciling common sense and intuition isn't always going to be easy at the moment, which is why you need to find quiet moments during which you can weigh things up more carefully.

18 MONDAY *Moon Age Day 5 Moon Sign Leo*

Present trends can work wonders for your intellect and make you as sharp as a pin when it comes to getting what you want by stealth. Not everyone appreciates your off the wall sense of humour but the people who understand you will think you are right on form and will revel in your company.

19 TUESDAY *Moon Age Day 6 Moon Sign Virgo*

This might not be an altogether comfortable day for the Archer. There is lots to be done and a strong possibility that you are trying to sort out too many situations at the same time. This is difficult, even for you and it might be necessary to drum up a little support if you are not going to lose the plot altogether.

20 WEDNESDAY *Moon Age Day 7 Moon Sign Virgo*

You tend to be very supportive of your friends and will also be offering significant assistance to family members. Younger people seem to be drawn to you at the moment, probably because Sagittarius is an ageless zodiac sign and doesn't suffer from a generation gap. The advice you offer can be of tremendous importance now.

21 THURSDAY *Moon Age Day 8 Moon Sign Libra*

This ought to be another good day and one during which you have a greater ability to please yourself – as well as satisfying others on the way. Family members are actively turning to you at the moment and you continue to be a fount of good advice. Strong social trends support you later in the day and could make for a good evening.

22 FRIDAY *Moon Age Day 9 Moon Sign Libra*

Positive thinking is essential if you want to knock down a few hurdles that have been surrounding you for some time. When it comes to making money you can now have more success than has been the case for a while. What is less certain is how long you will manage to hold on to any cash that comes your way.

23 SATURDAY *Moon Age Day 10 Moon Sign Scorpio*

Where money is concerned, be just a little careful this weekend. Cash can flow through your grasp like water and for this reason alone it would be sensible to find something to do that costs you nothing at all. Routines can be quite tedious but in a family sense they may be necessary to give confidence to others.

24 SUNDAY *Moon Age Day 11 Moon Sign Scorpio*

You should have much energy for Sunday, though you won't want to expound it on practical matters and are likely to be primarily concerned with having fun. People you don't see often could be playing a more important role in your life now and you won't be tardy when it comes to handing out invitations.

25 MONDAY *Moon Age Day 12 Moon Sign Scorpio*

Issues from the past could surface now and not all of them will prove to be entirely comfortable. When it comes to practical matters you don't understand there are people around who will be more than willing to help you out. Of course they won't be of much assistance unless you seek them out and ask them.

26 TUESDAY *Moon Age Day 13 Moon Sign Sagittarius*

It might seem fun to improve your surroundings in some way and today offers you the chance to do just that. At the same time the lunar high positively demands that you find the time to have some fun with those you love. Get out of the house and enjoy what summer weather there may be. The fresh air will do you no end of good.

27 WEDNESDAY *Moon Age Day 14 Moon Sign Sagittarius*

Don't look a gift horse in the mouth. If life is working out well you probably should not question why this is happening. Part of the reason is the lunar high, which can bring new opportunities and the possibility of excitement that comes like a bolt from the blue. At work you now have some important answers and can put them to the test.

28 THURSDAY *Moon Age Day 15 Moon Sign Capricorn*

It should not be difficult to get on well with everyone right now. Your flexible personality can turn your mood in almost any direction you wish and could help you to make an important new friend. There are some real personalities around you at the moment and they help life go with a swing.

29 FRIDAY *Moon Age Day 16 Moon Sign Capricorn*

You might feel that not everyone is on your side today but you could be wrong in at least one case. Just because someone is rather critical of your ideas or actions does not mean they will fail to support you. Don't react harshly until you really know the score – in fact it would be best not to fall out with anyone today if you can avoid doing so.

30 SATURDAY *Moon Age Day 17 Moon Sign Capricorn*

Making a strong impression on the right sort of people might be very important today. You are investing a lot of energy in directions that interest you but you may well shy away from situations you don't care for. You think a lot about refined topics, and actively want to mix with people who are as bright as you are.

July

2018

Your Month at a Glance

(+) = Opportunities are around (−) = Be on the defensive (○) = Life is pretty ordinary

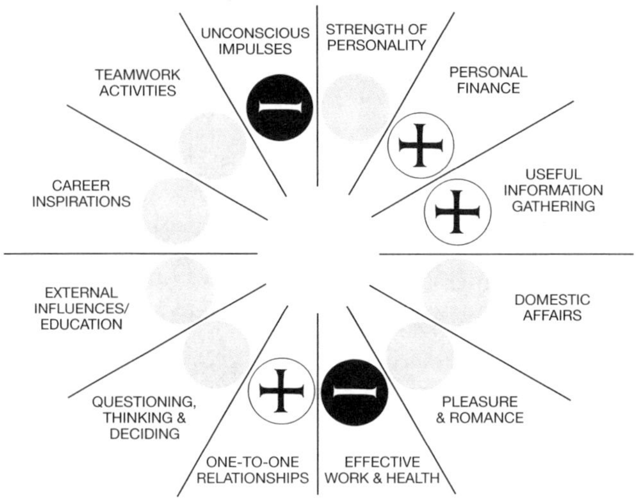

July Highs and Lows

Here I show you how the rhythms of the Moon will affect you this month. Like the tide, your energies and abilities will rise and fall with its pattern. When it is above the centre line, go for it, when it is below, you should be resting.

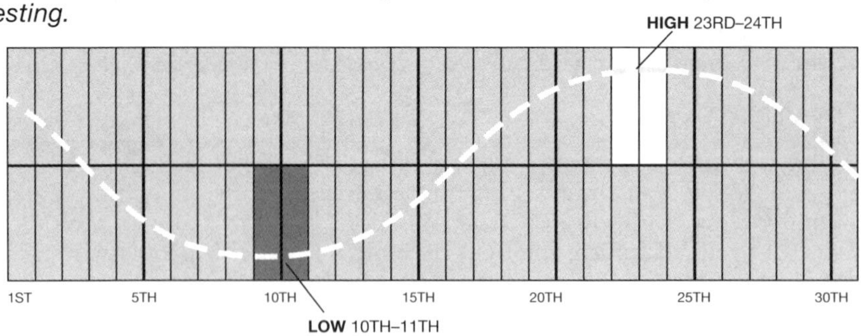

1 SUNDAY *Moon Age Day 18 Moon Sign Aquarius*

A change for the better may be coming along in your ability to communicate with others. It looks as though you will find it easier to persuade others of the virtues of your present plans. Even people who are generally rather sceptical are likely to be coming round to your point of view and this is mostly because you are so persuasive now.

2 MONDAY *Moon Age Day 19 Moon Sign Aquarius*

You want to feel more secure materially, even though you sometimes do silly things that are not likely to increase your bank account. With a mixture of favourable planetary influences it should now be easier for you to plan ahead and to stick to genuinely good ideas you have already had. Don't spend freely today.

3 TUESDAY *Moon Age Day 20 Moon Sign Pisces*

Now is definitely the right time to capitalise on your recent strategies and to move forward in a very progressive sense in terms of your work. If it has become obvious that you can't get what is owed to you in your present job you may be thinking hard about a total change. Think this through carefully before taking drastic action.

4 WEDNESDAY *Moon Age Day 21 Moon Sign Pisces*

There could be a few minor challenges on the domestic scene, some of which are likely to come about as a result of misunderstandings involving younger family members. Maybe you are at cross-purposes with someone or you cannot reach a necessary compromise? A little advice from outside the situation might help.

5 THURSDAY *Moon Age Day 22 Moon Sign Pisces*

As money matters are now set to improve somewhat, you are able to turn your mind in very different directions. Romance is a good place to start and if you are presently between relationships there are some very supportive planetary positions around now that would allow you to approach someone you really like with greater confidence.

6 FRIDAY *Moon Age Day 23 Moon Sign Aries*

Organisation is definitely the key to success for the Archer now and you can be really good at getting other people to do your bidding. It is important to concentrate on specific issues for the moment and not to go off at a tangent. People from the past could be coming into your life again, with some surprising results.

7 SATURDAY

Moon Age Day 24 Moon Sign Aries

There can be something deeply relaxing about today, and in fact the weekend as a whole. Find ways to enjoy the summer weather and make sure you get some good fresh air while circumstances allow. An outing with your partner or family members might appeal so pick somewhere that is truly beautiful.

8 SUNDAY

Moon Age Day 25 Moon Sign Taurus

Avoid situations today that mean you having to deal with endless details. It is the overview of life that appeals to you right now and you can leave the fine-tuning to everyone else. This would be a very good day to plan a trip or even to take a journey that has been planned at the last minute. As always you need change and variety.

9 MONDAY

Moon Age Day 26 Moon Sign Taurus

Since much now tends to be geared towards your home and the people it contains, you need to talk things through with your loved ones on a level you don't generally manage to do. Younger people especially are likely to have fixed opinions and whether you want to do so or not you need to take these fully on board.

10 TUESDAY

Moon Age Day 27 Moon Sign Gemini

This is likely to be a slack period and for this you can thank the lunar low. It doesn't matter how hard you try it will be virtually impossible to get up to speed, especially at work. Instead of bemoaning the fact, take time out to do some forward planning, and encourage others to work hard on your behalf if you can!

11 WEDNESDAY

Moon Age Day 28 Moon Sign Gemini

Time can hang heavy on your hands. This is rather strange for the Archer, which under normal circumstances could do with forty-eight hours in each day. If there are moments to spare you could occupy yourself with something creative and more intellectual than the subject matter you are generally expected to deal with.

12 THURSDAY

Moon Age Day 29 Moon Sign Cancer

Your thinking now takes you well ahead of many of the people you mix with on a daily basis and this could lead to a sense of superiority that is not really justified. Perhaps you are the expert in some ways, but no matter how tedious it may seem, other people can have good ideas too. It would benefit you to take these on board.

13 FRIDAY *Moon Age Day 0 Moon Sign Cancer*

Maximise your potential in monetary terms by spreading your resources around a little. Concentrating too much effort in one fiscal direction leaves you open to sudden fluctuations, which must be avoided at this time. If you have any doubt at all today, keep your wallet closed for a day or two.

14 SATURDAY *Moon Age Day 1 Moon Sign Leo*

When it comes to loved ones and the way you view them this should be a secure and happy phase of the month. Although you remain busy out there in the wider world you will also be turning your attention much more in the direction of your home and family than has been the case recently. You want to make everyone happy at present.

15 SUNDAY *Moon Age Day 2 Moon Sign Leo*

Go for peace and quiet at home, though this may be troubled by a sort of dissatisfaction within yourself, possibly because you are not making the sort of progress you would wish at the present time. Your options might be limited by situations you can't control and that is likely to frustrate you even more.

16 MONDAY *Moon Age Day 3 Moon Sign Virgo*

Life should prove to be very streamlined today and you should find yourself getting to your various destinations well ahead of schedule. The Archer doesn't take kindly to being pushed around at the moment and you will have little or no patience with rules and regulations that you see as pointless.

17 TUESDAY *Moon Age Day 4 Moon Sign Virgo*

You want to get down to the real nitty-gritty today but the problem might be that other people do not. As a result you will be flailing about somewhat and might become slightly anxious because you can't control certain situations. Try to adopt a more relaxed attitude and look deep inside yourself to find patience.

18 WEDNESDAY *Moon Age Day 5 Moon Sign Libra*

It is at this stage of July that domestic matters tend to take a centre-stage position in your thinking and actions. Relatives are anxious to learn your opinions and your partner should be very attentive and more than willing to listen to what you have to say. For some Archers this can also be a time to foster new romance.

19 THURSDAY *Moon Age Day 6 Moon Sign Libra*

You want to improve your lot at home but at the same time probably won't have quite the staying power necessary to put new plans into action. Travel may especially appeal to you at the moment. Even if you can only make the shortest of journeys today the results should be more than pleasing.

20 FRIDAY *Moon Age Day 7 Moon Sign Libra*

What a great time this would be for a holiday and those Sagittarians who planned to take one now were certainly inspired. Even if you have to work as usual, you could do with getting a short break. A walk by the sea or a little trip out into the country after work might be enough to make you feel really good.

21 SATURDAY *Moon Age Day 8 Moon Sign Scorpio*

New social interests could come your way during this weekend and today will also offer you the chance to break the bounds of the normal and to do something completely different. The attitude of friends will be warm and people can't seem to do enough for you. Don't get hung up on domestic details.

22 SUNDAY *Moon Age Day 9 Moon Sign Scorpio*

With boundless physical energy you present a positive face to the world. Friendships are very important at the moment but not nearly as significant as personal attachments. Romance flourishes under present trends and you have everything you need to make this a blissful and exciting personal interlude.

23 MONDAY *Moon Age Day 10 Moon Sign Sagittarius*

Now you begin to come into your own and you should notice how much more compliant those around you seem to be. Part of the reason for this is your own level of confidence, which inspires trust in others too. You certainly won't be stuck for the right thing to say under these trends and people will naturally warm to you.

24 TUESDAY *Moon Age Day 11 Moon Sign Sagittarius*

This is probably the best day of the month for pushing your luck and for moving forward progressively with plans that have been on hold for some time. Most of these are likely to be domestic or personal in nature and there could be one or two restrictions placed upon your professional progress. Enjoy an adventurous Tuesday.

25 WEDNESDAY *Moon Age Day 12 Moon Sign Capricorn*

Work matters might put you under a certain amount of pressure today but this is nothing you find difficult to deal with. Other people, those who believe you hold all the information, are also seeking you out. Of course you don't but it would be a pity to spoil the illusion. In most situations you will be able to dream up some sort of magic.

26 THURSDAY *Moon Age Day 13 Moon Sign Capricorn*

You are fairly fortunate in your dealings today – mainly because you present a capable face to the world and won't allow anyone to steal a march on you. It is possible for you to hang on to cash to a greater extent than would normally be the case and you are also using money to work on your behalf in a positive way.

27 FRIDAY *Moon Age Day 14 Moon Sign Capricorn*

You tend to surround yourself with very dynamic people at the moment, so that even when you are stuck for an idea your friends will not be. Co-operating should be very easy and you work well when in a think-tank sort of situation. You love word games at the moment and will be fascinated by poems, puzzles and fanciful tales.

28 SATURDAY *Moon Age Day 15 Moon Sign Aquarius*

Your intuition is strong and it is worth looking deep inside the motivations of others today in order to assess how they are likely to behave. This is something you need to know in order to plan your own actions and so you don't get left behind. You will not take kindly to being ordered about and if anything you react against it more than usual.

29 SUNDAY *Moon Age Day 16 Moon Sign Aquarius*

You seem to need constant mental stimulation today and won't be happy unless you are solving one problem or another. It isn't really the puzzles in the Sunday papers that appeal to you but rather those thrown up by life itself. It looks as though you have your detective head on and you are also yearning to see new sights.

30 MONDAY *Moon Age Day 17 Moon Sign Pisces*

If you really want to succeed at the start of this working week you will need to make even more of an effort than usual. However, the result is directly proportional to your actions, so that the harder you try the greater the rewards will be. You may also get the chance to test the loyalty and competence of colleagues.

31 TUESDAY

Moon Age Day 18 Moon Sign Pisces

You get on especially well now with cultured or even refined people and you will be happy when dealing with those who are naturally quiet and willing to get on with things without any fuss. Your attitude with colleagues might be a little guarded if you feel that you are being taken for granted or used in some way.

August

2018

Your Month at a Glance

+ = Opportunities are around — = Be on the defensive = Life is pretty ordinary

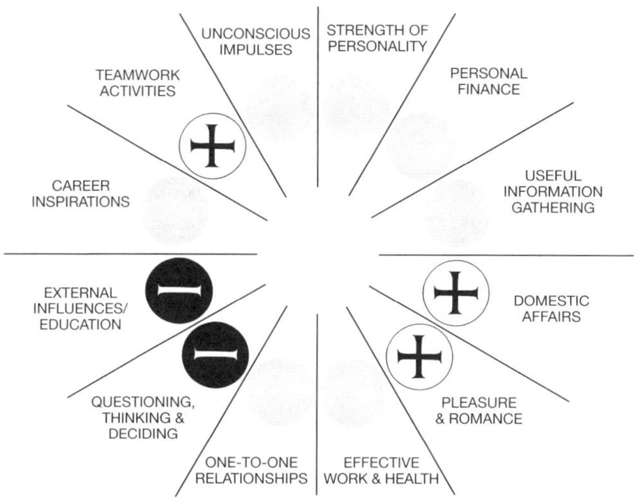

August Highs and Lows

Here I show you how the rhythms of the Moon will affect you this month. Like the tide, your energies and abilities will rise and fall with its pattern. When it is above the centre line, go for it, when it is below, you should be resting.

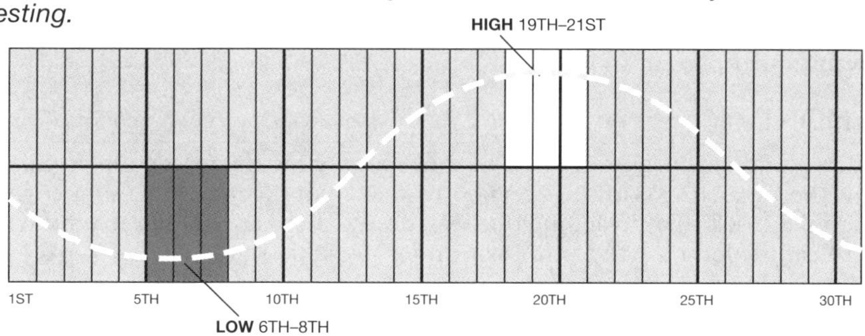

1 WEDNESDAY ☿ *Moon Age Day 19 Moon Sign Pisces*

It might be slightly difficult to get yourself moving at the start of this particular Wednesday. There will be small pressures around you that make it difficult to see your way forward as you would wish. Take on board what your colleagues and friends have to say because some of it is likely to be very sound advice indeed.

2 THURSDAY ☿ *Moon Age Day 20 Moon Sign Aries*

Activity remains essential and you won't be pleased if people or circumstances try to keep you in one place. You would be especially annoyed if you have to look at finances or read endless documents, no matter how important they might be. There is only one word that occupies your mind on this day and that word is freedom.

3 FRIDAY ☿ *Moon Age Day 21 Moon Sign Aries*

In the search for personal fulfilment you take the starring role in all social situations. There are gains to be made on the financial front but these could be minor and in some way short-lived unless you consolidate your actions. Life is a mixed bag at the moment but when it really matters your personality is certain to shine through.

4 SATURDAY ☿ *Moon Age Day 22 Moon Sign Taurus*

Your attention now turns in the direction of personal security. This means consolidating your finances and finding new ways to move money from one place to another. New personalities are likely to enter your life around now and some of these people threaten to outshine even you.

5 SUNDAY ☿ *Moon Age Day 23 Moon Sign Taurus*

It looks as though you will be quite provocative today and you won't shy away from discussions or even arguments if they seem to further your aims. This is the less acceptable side of the Archer because you can be manipulating and even scheming on occasions. It seems as though the end justifies the means under present trends.

6 MONDAY ☿ *Moon Age Day 24 Moon Sign Gemini*

Energy and enthusiasm may be in short supply for the next couple of days and the lunar low is almost certain to make you keener to sit in a corner and take stock than to act in your usual way. There are people around who are keen to lend a hand but even under present trends you may attempt to go it alone.

7 TUESDAY ☿ *Moon Age Day 25 Moon Sign Gemini*

You may prefer to keep your plans simple today and to avoid complicating issues that appear to be working out just fine on their own. This is certainly the preferred way to deal with the lunar low but because you are a Sagittarian you may still attempt to tamper and can make matters worse. By tomorrow more positive trends should return.

8 WEDNESDAY ☿ *Moon Age Day 26 Moon Sign Gemini*

You function best at the moment when you are called upon to communicate with those around you. You can have almost anything you want if you use a mixture of patience and well-considered words, though the former is harder to find than the latter. All seems settled and for the moment things look fine.

9 THURSDAY ☿ *Moon Age Day 27 Moon Sign Cancer*

Around this time you prove to be an excellent organiser and won't have any trouble at all in arranging social functions and gatherings of one sort or another. You will also be very charitably inclined and quite willing to do more than you normally might for those who are less well off than you are. Your social conscience is now very strong.

10 FRIDAY ☿ *Moon Age Day 28 Moon Sign Cancer*

It is likely that you will now begin to experience a degree of restlessness. There might seem to be nothing new about this in the life of the average Archer but your desire for change and diversity is now more intense. What makes matters slightly more difficult is that you won't be able to work out where the restlessness actually comes from.

11 SATURDAY ☿ *Moon Age Day 0 Moon Sign Leo*

Much energy is now channelled into practical projects and even work for those Sagittarians who have professional commitments at the weekend. You may be called upon to replace someone who is sick or away and the day could turn out quite differently from how you expect it to be at the start.

12 SUNDAY ☿ *Moon Age Day 1 Moon Sign Leo*

A time of great inspiration in your romantic and social life. When you are out of the house you will be effervescent and more than willing to join in with anything you see as being fun. At home you will be slightly quieter and more contemplative but you can you will be showing strong support for loved ones.

13 MONDAY ☿ *Moon Age Day 2 Moon Sign Virgo*

You will be forced to develop your inner resources around now because some of the usual structures on which you rely seem to be missing or inefficient. You can surprise yourself with your resilience in a number of different areas of life and in addition to helping yourself you can be of great use to just about anyone you encounter.

14 TUESDAY ☿ *Moon Age Day 3 Moon Sign Virgo*

Money-wise there could be a small improvement in your personal circumstances but don't expect to suddenly become rich. Both for now and for some days to come, look carefully at the way you are spending cash and make sure you always get the best value for money possible.

15 WEDNESDAY ☿ *Moon Age Day 4 Moon Sign Libra*

It is unlikely that you would enjoy working along only one track today and what you are most likely to be looking for is variety. Whilst others struggle to keep up you have what it takes to forge ahead and to show the world how capable you are. This ought to be a highly successful period and you are the master of your destiny now.

16 THURSDAY ☿ *Moon Age Day 5 Moon Sign Libra*

The Archer usually enjoys being in the limelight and this is certainly going to be the case today. There are likely to be a few practical pressures about but you will deal with these quite easily – especially if you ask a friend for some assistance. Some details of your social diary might have to be altered at the last minute.

17 FRIDAY ☿ *Moon Age Day 6 Moon Sign Scorpio*

Look for a smooth transition today, rather than a period during which you are racing away like a formula one car. You are neither too slow nor too careful in your approach but if you rush it is almost certain that mistakes will be made. Confidence is finely balanced at the moment and your ego can also be bruised rather easily.

18 SATURDAY ☿ *Moon Age Day 7 Moon Sign Scorpio*

Although today may start slowly it is only a matter of time before things speed up noticeably. There are new trends coming along that will positively affect the personal and domestic scene and you should find that life itself is looking after you very well. Is it good luck or good planning on your part?

19 SUNDAY *Moon Age Day 8 Moon Sign Sagittarius*

All the benefits of this fortunate time come flooding in and you will be on top form, no matter what you decide to do today. This would be the best time of all to be taking a holiday or for making trips for other reasons. The world can be your oyster so display all your natural verve and style.

20 MONDAY *Moon Age Day 9 Moon Sign Sagittarius*

Your innate curiosity is aroused by almost anything today and you will be turning over stones just to see what lies beneath them. People see you as being inspirational and ingenious, which is why they will be so keen to get on board with your many plans. Give yourself room to move and to breathe freely.

21 TUESDAY *Moon Age Day 10 Moon Sign Sagittarius*

Expect a few financial ups and downs at the moment and deal with these by taking the necessary action when you know you should. Delaying anything won't help at present and in any case you don't want to have too much on your mind. Sagittarius doesn't always face up squarely to its responsibilities but you can do so now.

22 WEDNESDAY *Moon Age Day 11 Moon Sign Capricorn*

Most of the truly rewarding moments you encounter today come along as a result of things that are happening at home. Relatives can prove to be quite charming and your partner especially so. Sagittarian subjects who are between romantic attachments at the moment can probably expect the most eventful midweek period of all.

23 THURSDAY *Moon Age Day 12 Moon Sign Capricorn*

Domestic responsibilities might get in the way of your need for personal freedom and, if so, you can expect to get a little tetchy about it. However, if you deal with thorny issues at home as soon as you can there should be plenty of time left during which to do whatever takes your fancy. Today is good for travel.

24 FRIDAY *Moon Age Day 13 Moon Sign Aquarius*

This could turn out to be a day of contrasts. While family issues are likely to be more settled, you could discover that you have practical problems you didn't expect. Some of these could be related to your work whilst others are to do with your inability to organise your social life in quite the way you would wish.

25 SATURDAY *Moon Age Day 14 Moon Sign Aquarius*

Intimate concerns and domestic duties could get in the way of you having a good time right now so it is worth taking some time out to spend on yourself. This is essential so that when you do turn your attention back towards family and home-based issues you do so with a clearer and more reasonable attitude.

26 SUNDAY *Moon Age Day 15 Moon Sign Aquarius*

You will be doing everything in your power now to stimulate some excitement and to get things moving, especially in a social and a romantic sense. Nudging life in the direction you want it to go will be no problem, though there are likely to be one or two people around who seem to resist your efforts at every turn.

27 MONDAY *Moon Age Day 16 Moon Sign Pisces*

At the start of a new working week you can expect to get ahead in the professional stakes and should be able to get one over on rivals. People see you as confident and well able to cope with any stresses and strains that come your way. It is actually the way you deal with problems that is the most impressive now.

28 TUESDAY *Moon Age Day 17 Moon Sign Pisces*

On the whole your domestic life is positively highlighted but there can be a few emotions that are rather too close to the surface, perhaps resulting from an incident either months or even years ago. This could be as good a time as any to get such matters out into the open and sort them out once and for all.

29 WEDNESDAY *Moon Age Day 18 Moon Sign Aries*

If you have been waiting for an important communication you can expect to be put out of your misery at any time now. It is important to keep your eyes and ears firmly open at present because new input is coming along from a range of different directions. It is important to vary your routines.

30 THURSDAY *Moon Age Day 19 Moon Sign Aries*

There seems to be many good things happening socially and the second to last day of August ought to offer significant gains for most Sagittarians. For many this turns out to be a pleasurable and self-indulgent sort of day and one during which you would relish the chance to get far away from ordinary life and routines that seem tedious.

31 FRIDAY

Moon Age Day 20 Moon Sign Aries

You now have the ability to convince anyone that you know what you are talking about. There is nothing especially surprising about this for the Archer but the trend is always welcome. It should be possible to help a friend today if they need advice, but also in overcoming any problem in their life.

September

2018

Your Month at a Glance

(+) = Opportunities are around (−) = Be on the defensive (○) = Life is pretty ordinary

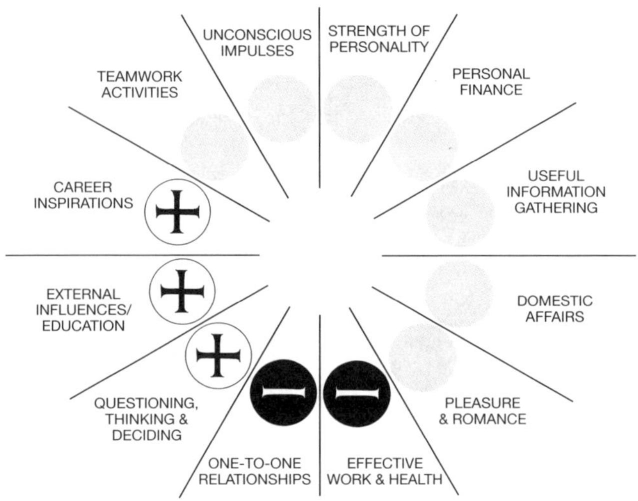

September Highs and Lows

Here I show you how the rhythms of the Moon will affect you this month. Like the tide, your energies and abilities will rise and fall with its pattern. When it is above the centre line, go for it, when it is below, you should be resting.

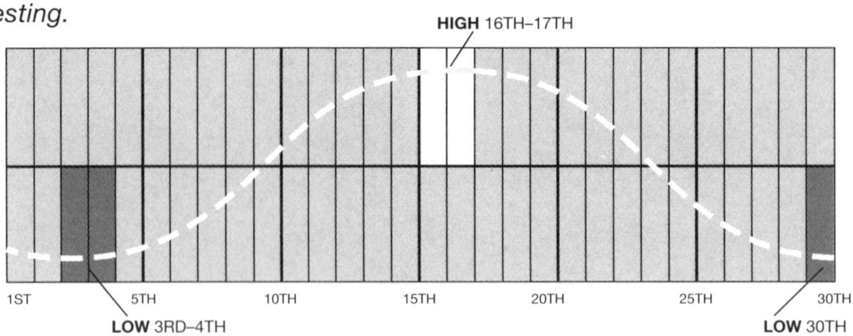

1 SATURDAY *Moon Age Day 21 Moon Sign Taurus*

This is a very dynamic social period for you and it looks as though the month of September could turn out to be quite memorable in a number of different ways. A little self-denial is possible today so it would be wise to hear what others have to say about you and to take notice of their comments.

2 SUNDAY *Moon Age Day 22 Moon Sign Taurus*

This would be a good day to be at home with your loved ones but that doesn't mean you are withdrawing from the world. Rather you are bringing life into your own abode and you could be entertaining friends or even strangers. All sorts of individuals hold a fascination for you at the present time, including a few very odd ones.

3 MONDAY *Moon Age Day 23 Moon Sign Gemini*

You can expect a few setbacks while the lunar low is around but it is unlikely that you will notice its presence too much if you take certain actions. For starters you need to withdraw into your own little world, and that means staying at home more than usual. You might also benefit from becoming involved in new hobbies or pastimes.

4 TUESDAY *Moon Age Day 24 Moon Sign Gemini*

It appears that you are still far more likely to stick to what you know than to push the bounds of the possible, at least until tomorrow. As a result you could find life to be slightly tedious and you won't have the level of energy you feel you need. Just be patient because everything will be back to normal in a day or two.

5 WEDNESDAY *Moon Age Day 25 Moon Sign Cancer*

Improved communication at home makes it possible for you to ask a relative for something that is quite important to you at this time. You have newer and better ways to make requests of others and your excellent talking skills certainly won't let you down. Double-check things to avoid unnecessary mishaps.

6 THURSDAY *Moon Age Day 26 Moon Sign Cancer*

Now you become more assertive at work and might be pushing for what you want, even if that means standing on the toes of colleagues. There is less of an inclination now for you to mix business with pleasure and your competitive instincts come to the fore.

7 FRIDAY *Moon Age Day 27 Moon Sign Leo*

A plan of action in the material world will require some thought before you commit yourself to it. Rush in recklessly is no way to proceed under present trends – though you could gain from listening to the advice of a family member. Others may now know more about you than you do yourself.

8 SATURDAY *Moon Age Day 28 Moon Sign Leo*

The more you adopt a broad-minded approach to life, the greater your awareness becomes. Things that remained hidden for so long now start to make sense and it looks as though you will also be let into some quite fascinating secrets. You seem to have your detective head on today and will be super inquisitive.

9 SUNDAY *Moon Age Day 0 Moon Sign Virgo*

The time is perfect to pursue new friendships and to get together with groups or associations that have not played a part in your life up to now. Whether for social or professional reasons you relish the prospect of meeting people face-to-face and you will love being the centre of attention. How can you fail to be happy right now?

10 MONDAY *Moon Age Day 1 Moon Sign Virgo*

Your professional lifestyle is now likely to be quite dynamic and peppered with incidents that keep you on your toes. Full of energy, you will relish almost as many challenges as life manages to throw in your path. Try a very new response to a very old problem and sort it out once and for all.

11 TUESDAY *Moon Age Day 2 Moon Sign Libra*

You can now find new ways to relate to others and will be on top form when socialising or sorting things out at work. The Archer is always keen to be in amongst people and this has never been more emphasised than it is at present. A new start is indicated at work, either a complete change or else an alteration in responsibilities.

12 WEDNESDAY *Moon Age Day 3 Moon Sign Libra*

A great love of life prevails and you will enjoy being in the limelight. This is as likely at work or in practical situations as it is on the social scene and you revel in good company at this time. In an optimistic mood, you may want to plan something special, most likely in order to spoil family members.

13 THURSDAY
Moon Age Day 4 Moon Sign Scorpio

Take full advantage of interesting chats with friends, or colleagues if you are at work. It's amazing how much you can learn at present by simply keeping yourself alert. Even when it appears that there is nothing to be gained you can ultimately find advantages in listening and talking. Don't try to achieve too much today.

14 FRIDAY
Moon Age Day 5 Moon Sign Scorpio

You should not have to work too hard today to achieve your objectives. Much of the preparatory work has already been done and this is likely to be a period for applying the finishing touches. Get in touch with people from the past and those who may be away from home at present.

15 SATURDAY
Moon Age Day 6 Moon Sign Scorpio

You are now at your very best when you can surround yourself with the comfortable and pleasant environment inside your home. There you will typically be entertaining visitors and making the most of a busy and satisfying family life. If this doesn't look remotely like you it is possible that you are doing something slightly wrong.

16 SUNDAY
Moon Age Day 7 Moon Sign Sagittarius

Now you should find major objectives going as planned and will only have to 'nudge' situations to get them moving in the right direction. The lunar high finds you riding on the crest of a wave and you will be keener than ever to make the sort of impression that is reserved for the Archer. People love you and that is what you really need.

17 MONDAY
Moon Age Day 8 Moon Sign Sagittarius

Attracting life's luxuries now becomes really easy and you will be happy to allow others to make a fuss of you. This is the perfect time for new starts and for getting to grips with previously complicated situations. Your powers of discrimination are good and you might also have luck on your side.

18 TUESDAY
Moon Age Day 9 Moon Sign Capricorn

What might set today apart is the feeling that you have the time to do whatever takes your fancy. Your schedule isn't likely to be rushed at the moment and that means you can get to grips with situations that have been waiting in the wings for a while. On the financial front you should be careful, but can spend a little if something takes your fancy.

19 WEDNESDAY *Moon Age Day 10 Moon Sign Capricorn*

There is now plenty of time available to think before you act. For the Archer this has to be a good thing because you are generally so inclined to simply launch yourself into any sort of situation with abandon. It is especially important now to analyse financial needs before you commit yourself to wholesale spending.

20 THURSDAY *Moon Age Day 11 Moon Sign Aquarius*

People will be happy to have you around and are unlikely to question either your motives or the decisions you make. They will look to you for leadership, even if it is only in terms of social situations. The autumn is approaching but there is still time to get out there and to enjoy what this most beautiful season has to offer.

21 FRIDAY *Moon Age Day 12 Moon Sign Aquarius*

It might feel as though something remains undone today – even if you cannot put your finger on what that might be. You are suffering from a state of anticipation but this should come as no surprise to you because this disease is a regular visitor to Sagittarius. Think carefully about just how well you can contribute to social situations now.

22 SATURDAY *Moon Age Day 13 Moon Sign Aquarius*

Your desire to know more and more could lead you up some unexpected roads today and you will be turning over stones wherever you go. There won't always be an end gain to your present curiosity - it's simply the sort of person you are. However, in the fullness of time everything you learn turns out to have some use in your life.

23 SUNDAY *Moon Age Day 14 Moon Sign Pisces*

Decision-making is made easy by the fact that many people are automatically willing to follow your lead. This may even extend to certain individuals who certainly haven't listened to your point of view so avidly in the past. You might even become slightly suspicious but the sort of reactions you are getting should be honest and genuine.

24 MONDAY *Moon Age Day 15 Moon Sign Pisces*

It should be easy to take the right decisions at work, though perhaps more difficult to know what to do domestically or romantically. Maybe you should have a chat with a friend, preferably a member of the opposite sex. They can give you opinions that would never have occurred to you on your side of the gender divide.

25 TUESDAY *Moon Age Day 16 Moon Sign Aries*

Look towards fulfilling as many practical objectives as you can today because in certain areas you may be falling behind your own targets. In particular, show colleagues and superiors that you are committed and fully in gear. It is likely to be the things you say rather than what you do that counts for the most at present.

26 WEDNESDAY *Moon Age Day 17 Moon Sign Aries*

Getting what you want from life today is merely a case of opening your mouth and asking for it. A little cheek can go a very long way and you are so naturally charming that people don't tend to refuse your requests. New possessions that come to you around this time might not be quite as appealing as you thought they would be.

27 THURSDAY *Moon Age Day 18 Moon Sign Aries*

Stand by for a slightly steadier sort of day and don't get too alarmed if you discover that you are much more emotional than usual at the moment. Certain situations can really move your heart and could see you taking on a charity commitment that will form at least a part of your life for a long time to come.

28 FRIDAY *Moon Age Day 19 Moon Sign Taurus*

Directness is very important in all situations that find you face to face with other people. Although you are naturally inclined to talk others round over a fairly long period, this is not going to work under present planetary trends. You have to tell it how it is, even if this goes against the grain for one or two individuals.

29 SATURDAY *Moon Age Day 20 Moon Sign Taurus*

Keep up the momentum for the moment because there will be time enough to rest later. You are now likely to encounter people who are naturally very deep and difficult to fathom. Turn on your intuition and let this be your guide in relationships. Common sense is important but it can only take you so far.

30 SUNDAY *Moon Age Day 21 Moon Sign Gemini*

As Sunday dawns you might be panicking about a commitment that is around the corner. It is best for the Archer not to worry too much in advance of situations but rather to make certain that everything is in place. After that, relax and turn your attention in other directions. You work hard and fast around now.

October

2018

Your Month at a Glance

(+) = Opportunities are around (–) = Be on the defensive ( ) = Life is pretty ordinary

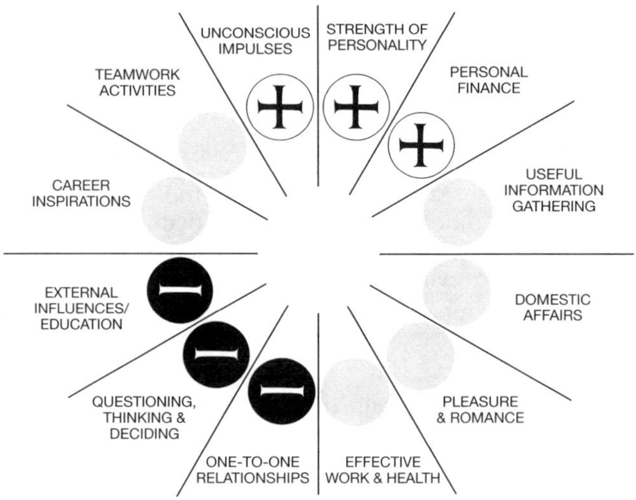

October Highs and Lows

Here I show you how the rhythms of the Moon will affect you this month. Like the tide, your energies and abilities will rise and fall with its pattern. When it is above the centre line, go for it, when it is below, you should be resting.

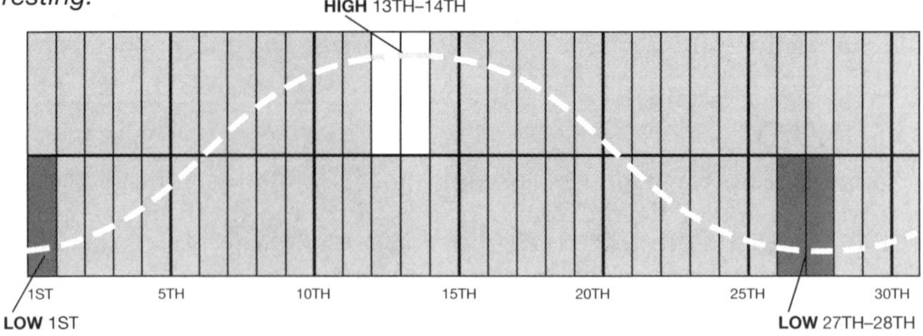

1 MONDAY
Moon Age Day 22 Moon Sign Gemini

Now the lunar low is well under way and this coincides with the start of a new working week. It would be advisable to move slowly and cautiously today and not to get too involved in situations you don't really understand. Learning on the job is part of what Sagittarius is about but the technique may not work too well for the moment.

2 TUESDAY
Moon Age Day 23 Moon Sign Cancer

In professional relationships it is now important for you to cultivate a more tolerant attitude. It could be that people are doing things that seem certain to irritate you though part of the problem could be coming from you. No such worries seem to exist in a more personal sense. You are warm and loving for most of the time.

3 WEDNESDAY
Moon Age Day 24 Moon Sign Cancer

Now you are especially sensitive regarding the impression you make on those around you – and much more so than would generally be the case. This does have a down side because for much of today it could feel as though you are walking on eggshells. Perhaps you are worrying too much. People are more resilient than you think.

4 THURSDAY
Moon Age Day 25 Moon Sign Leo

Your strengths today lie in love and all romantic matters. You have all it takes to be wonderful in the eyes of someone you count as being very special. For those Sagittarians who are not in a relationship at the moment it would be worth keeping your eyes open because Cupid is definitely about.

5 FRIDAY
Moon Age Day 26 Moon Sign Leo

Focus your sights on the romantic arena because you are still well able to turn heads and the effect you have on others is noteworthy. Part of the reason for this is your ability to become whatever is necessary under any given circumstance. Leopards might not be able to change their spots but for an Archer it is child's play.

6 SATURDAY
Moon Age Day 27 Moon Sign Virgo

You may now begin to enjoy a new sense of freedom. There could be less clutter in your life, partly brought about by your ability to ignore or dispose of issues that are no longer relevant to you. If you find yourself involved in any situation that involves confrontation you could discover that you are somewhat braver than you realised.

7 SUNDAY *Moon Age Day 28 Moon Sign Virgo*

When it comes to the practical side of life there is a sense that new things are happening all the time. This keeps you involved and interested, which is far better than allowing yourself to become bored with the same old routines. If you had begun to slightly doubt your popularity today's evidence should set you straight.

8 MONDAY *Moon Age Day 29 Moon Sign Virgo*

Opportunities now exist to get ahead in job-related matters. At the same time there is just a chance that you are getting carried away with your own sense of purpose and you won't suffer fools gladly. The only problem lies in the fact that all the judgements are yours and it might turn out that someone is not being in the least foolish.

9 TUESDAY *Moon Age Day 0 Moon Sign Libra*

Increased activity in your social life mirrors what is taking place at work and, all in all, you are likely to be getting busier and busier. That's fine as long as you don't run yourself ragged in your desire to achieve everything that is possible. Try to find time today to get in touch with friends who might have slipped from sight of late.

10 WEDNESDAY *Moon Age Day 1 Moon Sign Libra*

If you want to make some of your dreams into reality you are now in the best possible position to do so. People close to you should be more than happy to lend a hand and they will also be willing to share some of your erstwhile fantasies. Travel may be uppermost in your mind and get out and about freely today.

11 THURSDAY *Moon Age Day 2 Moon Sign Scorpio*

Do whatever you think is necessary today in order to get important people on your side. You are in a good position to get ahead in the practical world and all you need to complete the picture is a leg up from someone who has influence. Your charming nature should take care of the details and the rest is just a matter of flattery.

12 FRIDAY *Moon Age Day 3 Moon Sign Scorpio*

Right now there is a positive focus on material issues. You can build on fresh starts and will be able to demonstrate that you are certainly not a one-trick pony. Take note of good advice from friends and also try to put some time aside today to let your partner know you haven't entirely forgotten that they exist!

13 SATURDAY *Moon Age Day 4 Moon Sign Sagittarius*

Act now and ask questions later. It's true that the Archer is sometimes far too inclined to be impetuous but, for once, that should turn out to be a good thing. The lunar high means you will be charm itself and you are well able to get what you want when you need it. Good fortune is also likely to be on your side for today and tomorrow at least.

14 SUNDAY *Moon Age Day 5 Moon Sign Sagittarius*

You now have energy in abundance and no shortage of situations in which to use it throughout the whole day. People warm to your infectious enthusiasm and will be quite happy to be carried along with you. Not everything you dream up today will be practical in the longer-term but some of your ideas could run.

15 MONDAY *Moon Age Day 6 Moon Sign Capricorn*

Your tendency to be impulsive in your approach to others might take you just a little too far today, unless you exercise some control. There is a fine line between getting what you want and pushing people too hard. In most circumstances you walk that line with consummate professionalism but right now there is a chance you could fall off.

16 TUESDAY *Moon Age Day 7 Moon Sign Capricorn*

A mixture of tact and confidence makes your approach to others so good that they could hardly refuse you any reasonable request. As a result this is the best day of the week to ask for something you want – maybe a rise in salary or different working conditions. In any situation where you are explaining yourself you positively shine.

17 WEDNESDAY *Moon Age Day 8 Moon Sign Capricorn*

It looks as though you will be extremely busy today and won't have quite as much time to spend counselling others as both they and you might wish. All the same you will need to find a few moments to look after the interests of family members, as well as showing them that their needs and concerns are well understood.

18 THURSDAY *Moon Age Day 9 Moon Sign Aquarius*

There are good times on the way when it comes to getting on well at work. Some Sagittarians might be thinking about a total change of career but this may turn out to be unnecessary. The one thing you don't need this month is to become bored with your lot in life. Find some way to bring more excitement to your daily routines.

19 FRIDAY *Moon Age Day 10 Moon Sign Aquarius*

You won't want to do anything that goes against the grain today and will be quite happy to simply potter about in a way that suits you. That's fine as far as it goes but it doesn't take account of necessary responsibilities and the needs family members have of you. In some situations you will be far too casual and inclined to shrug things off.

20 SATURDAY *Moon Age Day 11 Moon Sign Pisces*

Look carefully at your finances this weekend and make any minor adjustments that seem necessary. For today you are active and enterprising but changes are on the way and so avoid taking on too much if it means putting in extra effort. Put a full stop to some issues right now.

21 SUNDAY *Moon Age Day 12 Moon Sign Pisces*

Sunday positively demands that you have fun and that you take other people with you on the roller coaster ride that is the Archer's life. For their part they should be more than willing to join in and there ought to be many laughs today. Socially and romantically you appear to have everything well sorted out.

22 MONDAY *Moon Age Day 13 Moon Sign Pisces*

There is no shortage of tasks to get your teeth into at the start of this week and you should be filled with a desire to get everything possible done. Of course there may be moments when you have to stop and think more clearly about specific issues, so rushing all the time could prove to be a negative approach.

23 TUESDAY *Moon Age Day 14 Moon Sign Aries*

Now fully committed to either career or education you learn quickly, adapt instantly and make the best of impressions on just about anyone. It will be necessary to do the things you don't want to do first – before you embark upon more enjoyable pursuits. Start early in the day and then you will have plenty of time for everything.

24 WEDNESDAY *Moon Age Day 15 Moon Sign Aries*

You can now be an inspiration to others and show by your attitudes and actions that you are a worthy role model. Avoid family arguments or even disputes with friends because once you start arguing now it is difficult for you to stop. Not everything is going to go your way on this particular Wednesday but the horizon looks good.

25 THURSDAY *Moon Age Day 16 Moon Sign Taurus*

The slightest thing you do for those around you is likely to be noticed and could be blown up out of all proportion as far as you are concerned. Nevertheless you will be popular and the social invitations are likely to roll in as a result. What you might really need is a rest but that can come later. For the moment just enjoy yourself.

26 FRIDAY *Moon Age Day 17 Moon Sign Taurus*

Give yourself fully to one task at a time and everything should turn out just fine. What you don't need is to have to start jobs all over again because they were not done properly. What's more you are being carefully monitored at present and will give a better impression of yourself if it is seen that you are efficient and exacting.

27 SATURDAY *Moon Age Day 18 Moon Sign Gemini*

You are unlikely to be up for new challenges now and will be happiest when you can simply plod along at your own chosen pace. The lunar low is almost certain to make you more emotionally responsive and you could feel as if there is nothing ahead that appears exciting. Don't react too strongly to what is a minor blip and nothing more.

28 SUNDAY *Moon Age Day 19 Moon Sign Gemini*

Perhaps you are still not giving of your best or feeling satisfied with life. As a result you could be moody and inclined to be pessimistic which is most unlike Sagittarius. Don't worry – very soon the clouds will clear, the lunar low will pass and a new week will bring an entirely different approach.

29 MONDAY *Moon Age Day 20 Moon Sign Cancer*

What really sets you apart at the moment is your huge and all-encompassing heart. Anyone who is in trouble or who needs timely advice could well be turning in your direction and will be grateful for your input. It might be suggested that the Archer is much better at sorting out the lives of others than it is at dealing with its own.

30 TUESDAY *Moon Age Day 21 Moon Sign Cancer*

Affairs of the heart are well accented under present trends and you should easily be able to make the sort of first impression for which Sagittarius is famous. Whoever you encounter today it will be possible for you to weigh up the pros and cons of their nature and to react accordingly. You should also be quite sporting around now.

31 WEDNESDAY *Moon Age Day 22 Moon Sign Cancer*

Some extra care is necessary over decisions at work, though socially it looks as though you are pushing ahead progressively and making a good impression on almost everyone. The result could be a series of new friends or an association with a group that hasn't played an important part in your life up to now.

November

2018

Your Month at a Glance

+ = Opportunities are around − = Be on the defensive ○ = Life is pretty ordinary

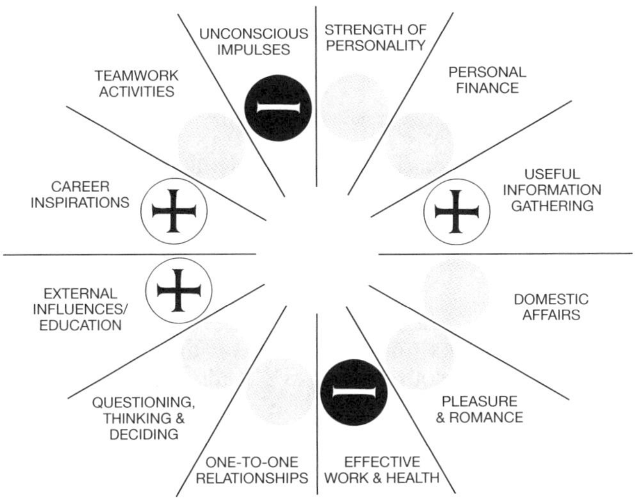

November Highs and Lows

Here I show you how the rhythms of the Moon will affect you this month. Like the tide, your energies and abilities will rise and fall with its pattern. When it is above the centre line, go for it, when it is below, you should be resting.

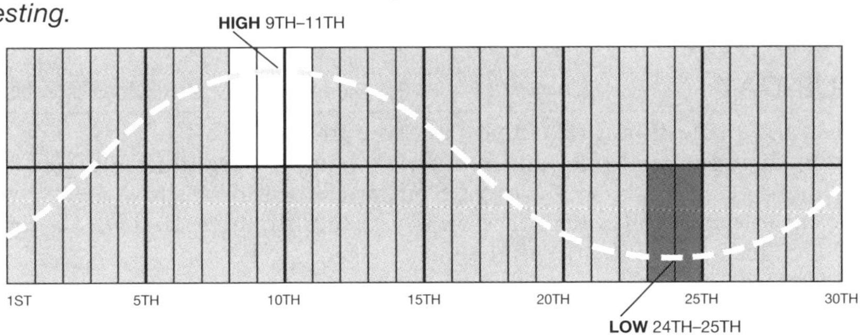

1 THURSDAY
Moon Age Day 23   Moon Sign Leo

Things are likely to be especially busy around your home and there might not be as much time as you would wish to commit yourself to the world outside. Relatives could be quite demanding and it won't be easy to fulfil everyone's expectations. Try to ring the changes as far as your social life is concerned.

2 FRIDAY
Moon Age Day 24   Moon Sign Leo

Take any opportunity that comes along to express yourself fully because otherwise there is a chance that people will fail to understand your reasoning or motivations. You can't be too truthful at the present time, even if you are a little worried that someone might think you are irrational or over-hasty.

3 SATURDAY
Moon Age Day 25   Moon Sign Virgo

Stand up for what you believe to be true and people will respect you much more than you might think. This weekend you could be faced with issues that need a swift resolution and nobody is better equipped to deal with the moment than you are. Look for a potentially warm and romantic evening to end a positive day.

4 SUNDAY
Moon Age Day 26   Moon Sign Virgo

Some personal attachments might seem to be more trouble than they are worth just at present. Of course this isn't really the case but it is true that even your partner might be causing you a degree of anxiety. Talk things through and accept that others may have a viewpoint that is sometimes far from your own. All that is needed is patience.

5 MONDAY
Moon Age Day 27   Moon Sign Libra

The interest you show in other people is noteworthy at the best of times but at the moment it is amazing. Nothing passes you by today and every nuance of life falls under your scrutiny. Some people might say you are nosey but in reality you only want to know what makes situations so fascinating and, of course, so diverse.

6 TUESDAY
Moon Age Day 28   Moon Sign Libra

Career and professional objectives are now much more likely to come to fruition than personal ones and you won't have any real difficulty getting your message across at work. Most Sagittarians will now show themselves to be capable and well able to take on new responsibilities. In truth though, not all colleagues will be on your side.

7 WEDNESDAY *Moon Age Day 0 Moon Sign Scorpio*

As always you are very tolerant towards those around you. Your 'live and let live' approach means that you rarely attract enemies but it can also get you accused on occasions of having no moral standards. This is not the case at all and you can prove at the moment how very human and humane you really are.

8 THURSDAY *Moon Age Day 1 Moon Sign Scorpio*

You have a talent for working in a one-to-one environment and you will be at your best today when you have to co-operate in order to make things work. There are times when you could be a little more competitive because you are sometimes too willing to settle for compromise all round. Finding the right balance is what today demands.

9 FRIDAY *Moon Age Day 2 Moon Sign Sagittarius*

Today the Moon returns to your zodiac sign and the lunar high offers all sorts of new incentives and possibilities you hadn't noticed before. Fortune takes you by the hand and guides you in the right direction and you are likely to be filled with a sense of fun from morning until night. You might confuse the lives of others but not your own.

10 SATURDAY *Moon Age Day 3 Moon Sign Sagittarius*

With boundless energy and a great determination to do everything you can to get ahead it is going to take people with real vitality to stay the course with you. Don't be too quick to point out the faults of others, especially since you might inadvertently be criticising yourself too. Keep relationships light and easy at this time.

11 SUNDAY *Moon Age Day 4 Moon Sign Sagittarius*

Avoid making spur of the moment purchases today and keep a tight hold on your money. Part of the problem is that Christmas is just around the corner, which is always expensive. Another stumbling block is that you might make what you think is an excellent buy, only to find the same item cheaper elsewhere.

12 MONDAY *Moon Age Day 5 Moon Sign Capricorn*

Your social life is extremely important to you; in fact it is sometimes difficult to know where other aspects of your life stop and social interaction begins. You will be especially good at mixing business with pleasure across the next few days and you can do yourself no end of good by maintaining good relations with colleagues.

13 TUESDAY *Moon Age Day 6 Moon Sign Capricorn*

Today you exhibit masses of charm but at the same time display a powerful personality. People that matter could be noticing you around this time and the fact that you are so inclined to persevere will not be lost on them. You might not realise that you are under scrutiny but it is likely to be taking place all the same.

14 WEDNESDAY *Moon Age Day 7 Moon Sign Aquarius*

There might not be time to do everything you had planned today but whether this is the case or not you do need to be certain that what you do is undertaken properly and efficiently. It is far more important for the moment to achieve your objectives in a limited way and that way you begin to see light at the end of a very long tunnel.

15 THURSDAY *Moon Age Day 8 Moon Sign Aquarius*

In your dealings with others you will probably show less self-control than would sometimes be the case. Sometimes you can be frank to the point of being rude and maybe a little more diplomacy would help. In particular, avoid getting on the wrong side of people who will soon be in a position to help you out.

16 FRIDAY *Moon Age Day 9 Moon Sign Aquarius*

What sets today apart? Well it looks as though you will be extremely sensitive and quite easily brought to tears. This is probably not on your own account but in response to the problems of others. You can even feel bad about something that is happening at the other side of the world but fortunately such trends don't last long for the Archer.

17 SATURDAY ☿ *Moon Age Day 10 Moon Sign Pisces*

With the weekend comes a desire to get things sorted out at home. If you are a DIY enthusiast you will now be tearing down walls, building new ones or redecorating. There is a strong spring-clean feeling about, which though odd for this time of year will make you feel better and when you feel better you act more spontaneously.

18 SUNDAY ☿ *Moon Age Day 11 Moon Sign Pisces*

All the love and devotion you can muster is now being heaped upon someone who is very special to you. Those little things that make all the difference come as second nature to you at the moment and making someone really happy is more or less what your life is about today. Try to smooth out disagreements at home.

19 MONDAY ☿ *Moon Age Day 12 Moon Sign Aries*

You want to have things just so, especially at home. 'A place for everything and everything in its place' is hardly your usual adage but seems to be so under present planetary trends. This might surprise those with whom you live and can also be a cause of no small amusement.

20 TUESDAY ☿ *Moon Age Day 13 Moon Sign Aries*

When it comes to the needs of relatives and friends you will probably be quite outspoken today and you won't take kindly to seeing anyone used or put upon. The Archer now decides that it has the solutions to the world's problems and will set out to put things right. That's fine in principle but slightly more difficult in practice.

21 WEDNESDAY ☿ *Moon Age Day 14 Moon Sign Taurus*

As far as work is concerned difficult jobs are done in a moment, while impossible ones could take just a little while longer. There could hardly be a better set of planetary circumstances when it comes to getting on well in life, though don't expect these trends to be with you indefinitely because there are hiccups.

22 THURSDAY ☿ *Moon Age Day 15 Moon Sign Taurus*

With some effort on your part you can reach destinations that seemed barred to you only a week or two ago. The change is probably in the attitude of those around you, some of whom are now much more willing to let you have your way. Don't get involved in arguments that have nothing to do with you.

23 FRIDAY ☿ *Moon Age Day 16 Moon Sign Taurus*

With one eye on the past and the other on the future you are able to learn from what you did before and to modify your stance as required. There are likely to be financial gains coming along all the time, even if these are small in size. What really matters is that you can make progress towards longer-term objectives.

24 SATURDAY ☿ *Moon Age Day 17 Moon Sign Gemini*

Put your biggest plans on the backburner and get some rest for the next couple of days. It isn't as if anything in particular is going wrong, merely that you don't feel as much like competing as might usually be the case. Your mind can wander far and wide but if you have the choice your body will be staying close to home.

25 SUNDAY ☿ *Moon Age Day 18 Moon Sign Gemini*

A brief time of withdrawal is still evident, though the lunar low this month can be turned to your advantage if only because it gives you more thinking time. With less stress around you can see things clearer than has been the case and that means that when the Moon moves on you will come out fighting straight away.

26 MONDAY ☿ *Moon Age Day 19 Moon Sign Cancer*

The more you throw in your lot with others during this part of the week the greater are the rewards that can come your way. It is true that you have to pay full attention at the moment and that you probably won't have quite the level of personal success you would wish but there is a good chance you are achieving more than you think.

27 TUESDAY ☿ *Moon Age Day 20 Moon Sign Cancer*

Go slowly today – not because there is any lack of energy or potential success but simply because the Archer is inclined to rush its fences and to fall occasionally as a result. The more circumspect you manage to be, the better is the chance that things will go your way. This is a time of opportunity and one that brings fun too.

28 WEDNESDAY ☿ *Moon Age Day 21 Moon Sign Leo*

Not every area of your life is equally productive at this time so take care about what you take on just now. Personal annoyance comes in your case from chasing a dream miles along the road, only to find it disappearing before your eyes. It's better to play for certainties than to indulge in pipe dreams.

29 THURSDAY ☿ *Moon Age Day 22 Moon Sign Leo*

Don't put off until another time what you can quite easily achieve now. People around you will be offering all sorts of possible diversions but there are jobs that need finishing and that has to come first. If you put down your tools now it will be more difficult to pick them up later and you may go down in the estimation of loved ones.

30 FRIDAY ☿ *Moon Age Day 23 Moon Sign Virgo*

There are a few challenges to be dealt with at work but it is likely you will take these in your stride and actually enjoy the cut and thrust of a fairly demanding interlude. In the main you should be on top form and more than willing to take on even more adventures once the demands of the working day are out of the way.

December

2018

Your Month at a Glance

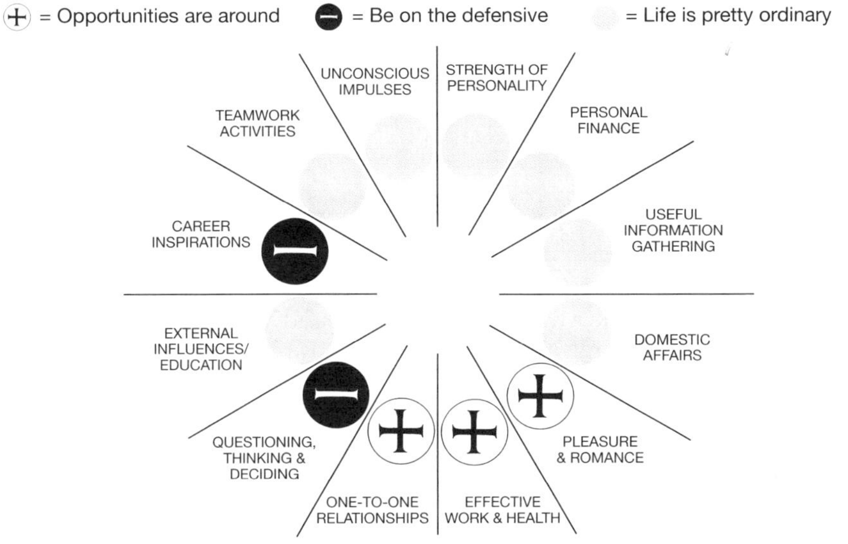

December Highs and Lows

Here I show you how the rhythms of the Moon will affect you this month. Like the tide, your energies and abilities will rise and fall with its pattern. When it is above the centre line, go for it, when it is below, you should be resting.

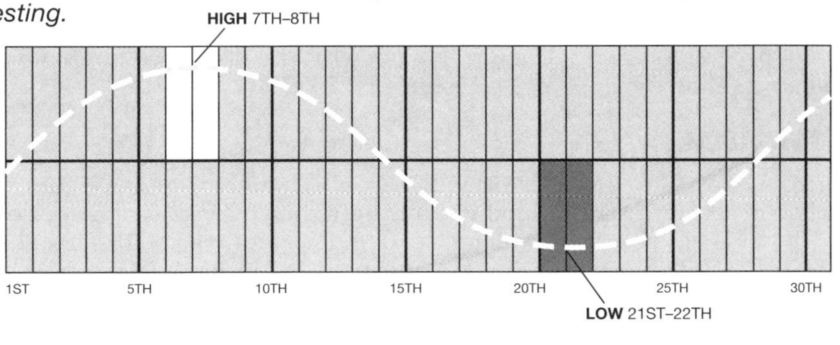

1 SATURDAY ☿ *Moon Age Day 24 Moon Sign Virgo*

Increased happiness can come from a gradually increasing feeling that you are now running your own ship. Sagittarius does not like to feel that someone else is totally in charge and you hate to be beholden to anyone. Today should offer significant social possibilities, most likely in the company of friends rather than relatives.

2 SUNDAY ☿ *Moon Age Day 25 Moon Sign Libra*

Your mind and your actions will turn more in the direction of those you love today. Although you are likely to retain your ability to get things right first time if you are at work, there are needs and wants coming from your relatives that will take up more of your time generally. Splitting your day could be problematic, but possible all the same.

3 MONDAY ☿ *Moon Age Day 26 Moon Sign Libra*

Creature comforts will be of relatively little importance right now and you will be more or less ignoring any need for greater security or forward planning. On the contrary you tend to make up your mind instantly and to think much more about what is happening around you now. In more than one way you want to forge ahead.

4 TUESDAY ☿ *Moon Age Day 27 Moon Sign Scorpio*

All decisions are now being made instantly and without too much recourse to the opinions of others. It isn't that you are insensitive – merely that you are sure of your position and remain certain that what is good for you will help those around you. That might well be true but you will need to explain it to them.

5 WEDNESDAY ☿ *Moon Age Day 28 Moon Sign Scorpio*

Today should be slightly better when it comes to your poise and balance. You gradually begin to take others into consideration, not simply in your mind but verbally too. The strange thing is that once you do explain yourself practically everyone will fall in line. It's not what you do that counts but how you go about it.

6 THURSDAY ☿ *Moon Age Day 29 Moon Sign Scorpio*

There are possible gains to be made today on account of your quick thinking and your desire to act on impulse. This isn't always the case of course but for the moment people are willing to fall in line with your thinking and to support you. Too many rules and regulations are inclined to get on your nerves at times like this.

7 FRIDAY *Moon Age Day 0 Moon Sign Sagittarius*

There should be no difficulty in getting what you want from life on this particular Friday. Having the lunar high around makes for a good way to end the working week, even if it also makes you rather more impatient than you perhaps should be. Play the hand you are holding for all you are worth because fortune is smiling on you now.

8 SATURDAY *Moon Age Day 1 Moon Sign Sagittarius*

A surplus of physical energy is to be expected and perhaps for the first time this year you are now fully into Christmas mode. Indeed, if invitations for celebrations are not coming your way today you are likely to create them for yourself. Getting others to play along should be really easy because you are tremendously persuasive today.

9 SUNDAY *Moon Age Day 2 Moon Sign Capricorn*

You now have powerful feelings about certain issues and you won't let things ride. There are many conversations possible and some of these are vital if you want to maintain full control over your own destiny. Others may be reminding you that Christmas is coming but you won't worry about that for a while.

10 MONDAY *Moon Age Day 3 Moon Sign Capricorn*

You should now be able to relax more in a professional sense. All the effort you put in previously is now likely to start paying dividends and you will be quite keen to make some major alteration with regard to the circumstances of your working life. At home you may be slightly annoyed by the strange behaviour of younger people.

11 TUESDAY *Moon Age Day 4 Moon Sign Aquarius*

You are now at your best when you are firmly ensconced in tasks that take up most of your effort and attention. It is the fine details of life that matter the most under present planetary trends and that is slightly unusual for Sagittarius, which usually concerns itself with the bigger picture and broader trends. Don't be too picky with relatives.

12 WEDNESDAY *Moon Age Day 5 Moon Sign Aquarius*

Expect friendly co-operation to be the order of the day when it comes to the professional side of your life, though this is less likely in a domestic or even a friendship sense. At the same time there are strong romantic signals in your chart so today turns out to be a mixed bag of both good and not-so-good trends.

13 THURSDAY
Moon Age Day 6 Moon Sign Aquarius

It may now be necessary to begin the reconstruction of certain parts of your life. There are gains to be made at the start of next year but the alterations necessary to get them will begin around now. Listen to the suggestions that are being made by colleagues and friends and don't dismiss a rather odd idea completely out of hand.

14 FRIDAY
Moon Age Day 7 Moon Sign Pisces

You know what you want to say today and won't have any difficulty at all getting your message across to others. The only slight fly in the ointment is that you could be rather too direct for some people and that could lead to arguments. There are times when you should be diplomatic and show sensitivity.

15 SATURDAY
Moon Age Day 8 Moon Sign Pisces

You may experience an increase in social engagements, which is of course to be expected so close to the festive season. All the same you want to concentrate on the practical side of life and won't take kindly to being shunted from pillar to post in order to please others. You can actually be quite cranky and awkward at the moment.

16 SUNDAY
Moon Age Day 9 Moon Sign Pisces

Some situations could seem irritating – even if the core of the problem is your own state of mind. You won't get everything you want simply by wishing it was so and extra effort will be necessary if you want to persuade others that you have all the answers. Get to grips with social demands before things get too hectic.

17 MONDAY
Moon Age Day 10 Moon Sign Aries

Laughter is truly the best tonic at the moment and you can really take the heat out of almost any situation with your cheerful and joking attitude to life. There are some slight financial gains on the way, even if these are only a realisation that you are slightly better off than you thought. Your confidence generally is beginning to grow.

18 TUESDAY
Moon Age Day 11 Moon Sign Aries

There are thoughts at the back of your mind that demand more of your attention today and you have what it takes to concentrate on things more than usual. Emotions could run high in the family and whether you realise it or not some of them are being jacked up by your own present attitude. Listen to younger people, especially today.

19 WEDNESDAY *Moon Age Day 12 Moon Sign Taurus*

Just remember that even the Archer cannot please all of the people all of the time. There are likely to be a few people around now who will remain dissatisfied with whatever you do. Instead of concentrating on the awkward types you should be looking towards the multitude that think you are the bee's knees.

20 THURSDAY *Moon Age Day 13 Moon Sign Taurus*

If there is some tension about today you can do a great deal to dissipate it merely by being your usual charming self. People love to have you around, partly because you are so good at entertaining them. You will be increasingly on show for the next few days, not just because of Christmas but also on account of changing planetary trends.

21 FRIDAY *Moon Age Day 14 Moon Sign Gemini*

There may be a few complications today and it would be sensible to proceed fairly cautiously at first. The lunar low can make you feel as though you are not totally in charge of situations but this really isn't the case and everything should turn out fine in the end. All the same, it might be safest to seek out professional advice on occasion.

22 SATURDAY *Moon Age Day 15 Moon Sign Gemini*

The ups and downs of everyday life will continue much as before but there is a sense that certain matters are changing now or are at least about to alter. Getting things working exactly as you would expect might not be all that easy at first and a good deal of application is needed if you want to feel fully in charge of your own destiny.

23 SUNDAY *Moon Age Day 16 Moon Sign Cancer*

In the main you are a leader and not a follower. This tendency is much enhanced at present and you could easily fall out with those who try to insist that you follow any course of action that is not inspired from within yourself. You need to be in command and this is the fact that is likely to cause you a few upsets around now.

24 MONDAY *Moon Age Day 17 Moon Sign Cancer*

Enjoy everything that Christmas Eve has to offer in the knowledge that almost everyone around you is happy and contented. That may also include you but under present trends there are bound to be things that seem too routine and inflexible. Curb your natural enthusiasm for upheaval, at least for Christmas.

25 TUESDAY
Moon Age Day 18 Moon Sign Leo

Christmas Day looks settled and there are trends about that indicate the possibility of meeting new people, so maybe you have decided to get out of the house at some stage. Whatever you decide to do you should be secure in the support and love of family members and especially your partner. Stand by for supersonic surprises.

26 WEDNESDAY
Moon Age Day 19 Moon Sign Leo

Now would be a good time for travel, even if you are only thinking in terms of short journeys to visit relatives or friends. You certainly will not want to stay at home throughout the whole Christmas period and will get bored unless you ring the changes in some way. You become more and more a party animal as the days progress.

27 THURSDAY
Moon Age Day 20 Moon Sign Virgo

Your ego is rather inflated, though there is nothing wrong about that as long as you use the trend constructively. There is just a slight possibility that you can upset others by being too abrupt or tactless, though this is something you can counter if you try.

28 FRIDAY
Moon Age Day 21 Moon Sign Virgo

From an emotional viewpoint you could be hanging on to issues and situations from the past that have little or nothing to do with your life at the moment. This is in sharp contrast to your more practical mind, which is proceeding without any interruption or delay. Two opposing attitudes at the same time might be somewhat confusing.

29 SATURDAY
Moon Age Day 22 Moon Sign Libra

Find the right people today – that is the most important advice whilst the Sun occupies its present position in your solar chart. It doesn't matter whether you need the chimney sweeping or if you want to organise a trip somewhere. There is always someone around who is an expert and you need to find that individual now.

30 SUNDAY
Moon Age Day 23 Moon Sign Libra

This is no time to gamble wildly on things turning out well simply because you want them to. What is required most at this particular time is better planning and a few trial runs. People generally should be fairly helpful but there will be one or two awkward people around who take more persuading than usual.

31 MONDAY

Moon Age Day 24 Moon Sign Libra

From a social point of view the world is definitely on your side today. Just be careful that you don't bite off more than you can chew. It might be best to keep the day generally quiet, so that by the evening you will be ready to party with the best of them. Sagittarius loves to party.

How to Calculate Your Rising Sign

Most astrologers agree that, next to the Sun Sign, the most important influence on any person is the Rising Sign at the time of their birth. The Rising Sign represents the astrological sign that was rising over the eastern horizon when each and every one of us came into the world. It is sometimes also called the Ascendant.

Let us suppose, for example, that you were born with the Sun in the zodiac sign of Libra. This would bestow certain characteristics on you that are likely to be shared by all other Librans. However, a Libran with Aries Rising would show a very different attitude towards life, and of course relationships, than a Libran with Pisces Rising.

For these reasons, this book shows how your zodiac Rising Sign has a bearing on all the possible positions of the Sun at birth. Simply look through the Aries table opposite.

As long as you know your approximate time of birth the graph will show you how to discover your Rising Sign.

Look across the top of the graph of your zodiac sign to find your date of birth, and down the side for your birth time (I have used Greenwich Mean Time). Where they cross is your Rising Sign. Don't forget to subtract an hour (or two) if appropriate for Summer Time.

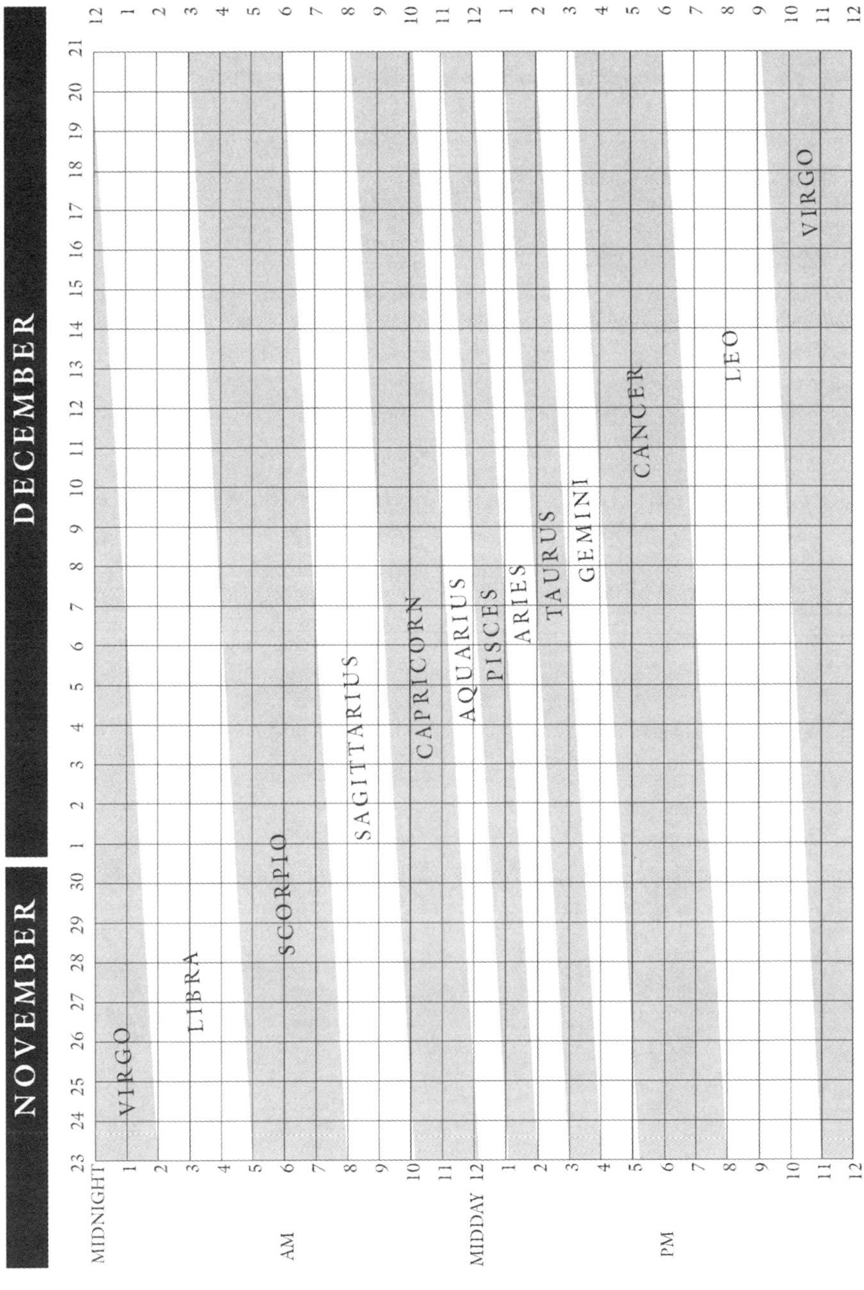
NOVEMBER
DECEMBER
MIDNIGHT
AM
MIDDAY
PM
VIRGO
LIBRA
SCORPIO
SAGITTARIUS
CAPRICORN
AQUARIUS
PISCES
ARIES
TAURUS
GEMINI
CANCER
LEO
VIRGO

THE ZODIAC, PLANETS AND CORRESPONDENCES

The Earth revolves around the Sun once every calendar year, so when viewed from Earth the Sun appears in a different part of the sky as the year progresses. In astrology, these parts of the sky are divided into the signs of the zodiac and this means that the signs are organised in a circle. The circle begins with Aries and ends with Pisces.

Taking the zodiac sign as a starting point, astrologers then work with all the positions of planets, stars and many other factors to calculate horoscopes and birth charts and tell us what the stars have in store for us.

The table below shows the planets and Elements for each of the signs of the zodiac. Each sign belongs to one of the four Elements: Fire, Air, Earth or Water. Fire signs are creative and enthusiastic; Air signs are mentally active and thoughtful; Earth signs are constructive and practical; Water signs are emotional and have strong feelings.

It also shows the metals and gemstones associated with, or corresponding with, each sign. The correspondence is made when a metal or stone possesses properties that are held in common with a particular sign of the zodiac.

Finally, the table shows the opposite of each star sign – this is the opposite sign in the astrological circle.

Placed	Sign	Symbol	Element	Planet	Metal	Stone	Opposite
1	Aries	Ram	Fire	Mars	Iron	Bloodstone	Libra
2	Taurus	Bull	Earth	Venus	Copper	Sapphire	Scorpio
3	Gemini	Twins	Air	Mercury	Mercury	Tiger's Eye	Sagittarius
4	Cancer	Crab	Water	Moon	Silver	Pearl	Capricorn
5	Leo	Lion	Fire	Sun	Gold	Ruby	Aquarius
6	Virgo	Maiden	Earth	Mercury	Mercury	Sardonyx	Pisces
7	Libra	Scales	Air	Venus	Copper	Sapphire	Aries
8	Scorpio	Scorpion	Water	Pluto	Plutonium	Jasper	Taurus
9	Sagittarius	Archer	Fire	Jupiter	Tin	Topaz	Gemini
10	Capricorn	Goat	Earth	Saturn	Lead	Black Onyx	Cancer
11	Aquarius	Waterbearer	Air	Uranus	Uranium	Amethyst	Leo
12	Pisces	Fishes	Water	Neptune	Tin	Moonstone	Virgo